BORDERLINE PERSONALITY DISORDER WORKBOOK

EXERCISES, TOOLS AND STRATEGIES

Jennifer C. Dove

McDove Publishing

Also by Jennifer C. Dove

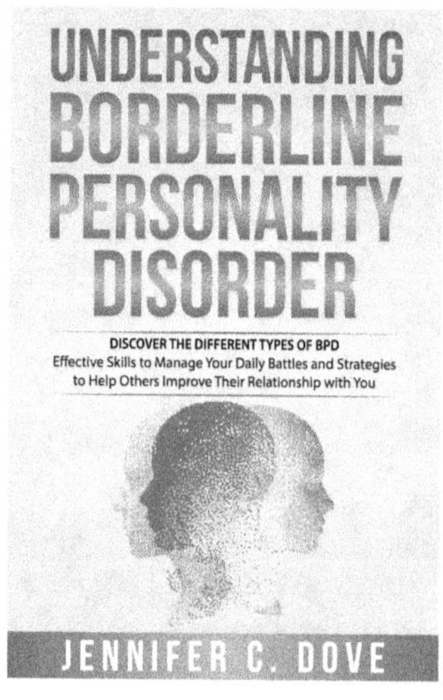

https://amzn.to/3GaNtDY

Contents

Introduction

Borderline Personality Disorder (BPD) presents a complex landscape of emotional volatility that demands daily navigation. The experience is often akin to walking a tightrope, where one misstep can lead to overwhelming emotions and instability. This condition affects approximately 1.4% of American adults, with a predominant diagnosis among women. The impact of BPD extends beyond the individual; it also profoundly affects relationships and personal identity, creating a pressing need for effective management strategies both for those diagnosed and their loved ones.

This guide is a practical companion to the book, Understanding Borderline Personality Disorder, providing actionable strategies to manage the disorder. It's designed for both individuals suffering from BPD and those supporting them, offering tools to enhance self-awareness, regulate emotions, and foster stable relationships.

As we explore this workbook, you'll be introduced to exercises and strategies tailored to improve emotional control and interpersonal relationships. This is more than a coping mechanism—it's a pathway to thriving despite the challenges of BPD.

One of the core struggles for those with BPD is identity disturbance, marked by profound uncertainty about self-identity. This may manifest as shifting goals and beliefs, making consistency in life a significant challenge.

To combat this, the workbook provides exercises that promote consistent self-image and clarity in personal values.

Fear of abandonment is another hallmark of BPD, often leading to problematic behaviors that strain relationships. You will find strategies to mitigate these fears through secure relationship-building techniques and effective communication practices here.

Workbook Overview

This workbook includes:

- Exercises: Engaging activities designed to teach skills like emotional regulation and interpersonal effectiveness.

- Reflections: Prompts to help you delve deeper into personal experiences and emotions.

- Strategies: Practical, step-by-step guides for managing BPD symptoms and improving relationship dynamics.

Benefits of This Workbook

- Enhanced Self-Understanding: Deepen your knowledge of BPD and its effects on thoughts and behaviors.

- Improved Emotional Regulation: Learn to manage intense emotions and respond to stress more healthily.

- Strengthened Relationships: Gain tools to improve communication, resolve conflicts, and build more robust relationships.

- Empowerment and Personal Growth: Equip yourself with skills to take control of your mental health and personal development.

Embark on this journey with clear, achievable goals using the SMART framework—Specific, Measurable, Achievable, Relevant, and Time-bound. Reflect on your challenges and define success in areas like emotional regulation or relationship stability. Regularly revisit these goals, adjusting them as necessary to align with your experiences and insights gained from this workbook.

Your path to a balanced and empowered life starts now. Use this workbook as your guide and return to it whenever you need a refresher. Your commitment to applying these strategies will transform your approach to managing BPD.

Note: You may want to jump to a particular chapter, but I recommend you follow the chapters in the order they are presented to you.

Additionally, you might want to consider keeping a notebook or journal on hand to complete the exercises.

Chapter One
Exploring Borderline Personality Disorder Together

Sarah had always been the life of the party, quick to laugh and the first to cry. Her emotions, like fireworks, were beautiful yet fleeting, and those closest to her often found themselves walking on eggshells, unsure which Sarah they would encounter from one moment to the next. During a routine session, her therapist introduced the term "Borderline Personality Disorder" (BPD). The name seemed like a label that didn't fit, too clinical for the storm of emotions she felt inside. Yet, as her therapist began to describe the symptoms, Sarah felt a sense of relief wash over her. Finally, there was a name for the roller coaster she had been riding alone for so long.

Borderline Personality Disorder is a mental health condition marked by a pattern of ongoing instability in moods, behavior, self-image, and functioning. These experiences often result in impulsive actions and unstable relationships. Individuals with BPD may experience intense episodes of anger, depression, and anxiety that can last from a few hours to days. Recognizable signs include emotional unpredictability, a constantly changing self-image, frantic efforts to avoid real or imagined abandonment, and a tendency to see things in extremes—either all good or all bad.

The complexity of BPD lies in its very nature: a whirlwind of emotions that can change direction without a moment's notice. Imagine feeling every emotion on a magnified scale, where a slight remark can spiral into a storm of self-doubt, or joy can quickly crash into despair. This intensity doesn't just affect the person with BPD; it ripples out to touch everyone in their life.

As Sarah sat across from her therapist, she realized that understanding BPD wasn't just about putting a name to her feelings; it was about starting a journey toward self-understanding and healing. It was about recognizing that, while her emotions could be overwhelming, they did not define her. Instead, they were sometimes confusing signals but always pointing towards the deep, underlying currents of her heart and mind. With this new understanding, Sarah felt a glimmer of hope. For the first time, she saw a path forward, not just for herself but for all those who had been misunderstood like her.

What is Borderline Personality Disorder?

Borderline Personality Disorder (BPD) unravels as a complex condition, profoundly affecting one's emotions, relationships, and sense of self. Grasping its nuances becomes crucial, not just for those diagnosed but for anyone entwined in their lives. This mental health condition throws a spotlight on the urgent need for clarity and comprehension. With symptoms that weave through the fabric of daily life, impacting decisions, relationships, and self-image, understanding BPD is the first step towards managing its profound effects. The following sections delve into the symptoms and impacts of BPD, providing a clear, precise foundation for our exploration.

Definition and Symptoms

Borderline Personality Disorder stands at the crossroads of complexity and misunderstanding in mental health. It's a condition characterized by an intense variability in mood, self-image, and behavior, which can lead to significant distress or impairment in personal, social, or occupational situations. Central to BPD is the struggle with emotional regulation, where feelings can swing unpredictably from one extreme to another.

Here are the key symptoms, broken down into clear, understandable language:

- Intense mood swings: Feelings can change drastically within a few hours or days, from extreme happiness to deep sadness or anger, without an apparent reason.

- Uncertainty about oneself: A person's self-image, goals, and even sexual orientation can change frequently. This instability can lead to sudden changes in jobs, friendships, values, or aspirations.

- Extreme reactions to abandonment: Real or imagined fears of being left alone can trigger intense reactions. This fear often leads to desperate attempts to keep relationships.

- Pattern of unstable relationships: Relationships may be characterized by alternating between extremes of idealization and devaluation (sometimes referred to as "splitting"), meaning the person with BPD may see others as either entirely perfect or flawed.

- Impulsive behaviors: This might include reckless driving, binge eating, substance abuse, or spending sprees. These actions are often taken without a thought for the consequences.

- Self-harming behaviors and suicidal threats or actions: Acts of self-injury, such as cutting or threats of suicide, can occur, especially in response to fear of separation or rejection.

- Chronic feelings of emptiness: A pervasive sense of emptiness or boredom that people with BPD struggle to describe.

- Inappropriate, intense anger: Difficulty controlling anger can lead to explosive outbursts or ongoing resentment.

- Feeling disconnected from oneself or reality: Experiences of feeling detached from one's body or thoughts of the world around them (dissociation).

Understanding these symptoms is vital for recognizing BPD in oneself or others and fostering empathy and support. The complexity of BPD symptoms demands an approach rooted in compassion and a readiness to seek understanding beyond the surface.

Personal Reflection: Identifying Your Connection with BPD

Discovering your personal connection can illuminate your understanding of yourself and the disorder more deeply. Whether you've been diagnosed with BPD, suspect you might have it or are supporting someone who does, reflecting on your experiences can provide invaluable insights and foster a greater sense of empathy and connection.

Consider these reflective questions to explore your relationship with BPD. Allow yourself to answer honestly, and if possible, jot down your thoughts and feelings. This exercise is not about right or wrong answers but rather understanding your unique perspective and experiences.

- What led you to pick up this workbook? Was it a diagnosis, the experience of someone close to you, or simply curiosity? Identifying your motivation can help clarify what you hope to gain from this journey.

- Reflect on your initial reactions to hearing about BPD. How have your thoughts and feelings about BPD evolved since then? Acknowledging changes in your perception can highlight your learning and growth.

- Can you recognize any BPD symptoms in yourself or someone close? Describing these without judgment can be the first step towards compassion and understanding.

- How has BPD touched your life or that of someone you care about? Consider the impact on relationships, work, and well-being. Recognizing these effects can guide your focus as you navigate the workbook.

- Identify your most significant challenges related to BPD. Whether they are emotional, relational, or practical, understanding these challenges can help prioritize your goals.

- Have you faced misunderstandings or judgments about BPD? Reflecting on these moments can shed light on the stigma surrounding the disorder and inspire resilience.

- What do you hope to achieve by completing this workbook? Setting intentions can motivate your journey and provide a roadmap for your exploration.

- Think about your support network. How comfortable do you feel discussing BPD with friends, family, or professionals? Recognizing the strengths and limits of your support system is crucial for finding additional resources and understanding.

Engaging with these questions honestly can mark the beginning of a meaningful exploration into BPD, offering perspectives that enrich your understanding and foster empathy for those affected by the disorder.

Activity: BPD Awareness Quiz

Test your knowledge and uncover the truths behind common misconceptions about Borderline Personality Disorder. This quiz invites you to challenge what you think you know, learn something new, and break down the barriers of stigma surrounding BPD. For each statement, decide if it's a fact or a myth, then check the explanations for insights.

1. BPD is rare and hardly affects the general population.

   - Myth. BPD affects approximately 1.4% of adults. It's more common than many realize, highlighting the importance of understanding and awareness.

2. People with BPD cannot have healthy relationships.

   - Myth. While BPD can challenge relationships, with appropriate therapy and support, individuals with BPD can foster strong, healthy connections.

3. BPD symptoms are just an extreme version of normal emotions.

   - Myth. BPD symptoms go beyond normal emotional reactions.

They involve intense and prolonged emotional states that can significantly impact a person's life.

4. Only women are diagnosed with BPD.

- Myth. Although BPD is more frequently diagnosed in women, it also affects men. Gender differences in diagnosis may reflect societal biases rather than actual prevalence rates.

5. There is no effective treatment for BPD.

- Myth. Several treatments, such as Dialectical Behavior Therapy (DBT), have been proven effective in managing BPD symptoms and improving quality of life.

This quiz is a step towards demystifying BPD, encouraging a deeper understanding and empathy for those affected by it. By confronting these misconceptions, we pave the way for a more informed and compassionate dialogue about mental health.

Activity: Personal DSM-5 Checklist

Embark on a journey of self-discovery with this simplified checklist based on the Diagnostic and Statistical Manual of Mental Disorders, Fifth Edition (DSM-5), criteria for Borderline Personality Disorder. Before you begin, remember this tool is meant for reflection and education. It cannot replace the nuanced understanding and diagnosis a professional can provide. If you recognize several of these symptoms in yourself or someone close to you, consider reaching out to a healthcare provider for a comprehensive evaluation.

BPD Symptom Checklist:

1. Emotional Instability: Do you experience intense mood swings over minor incidents lasting a few hours to a few days?

2. Fear of Abandonment: Is there a persistent fear of being left alone, leading to drastic measures to avoid real or imagined separation or rejection?

3. Unstable Relationships: Are your relationships marked by alternating extremes of idealization and devaluation?

4. Unclear or Shifting Self-Image: Do you struggle with your identity or self-image, experiencing significant shifts in self-identity, values, or aspirations?

5. Impulsive Behaviors: Have you engaged in impulsive behaviors that are potentially self-damaging, such as reckless driving, binge eating, or substance abuse?

6. Self-Harm: Have there been recurrent suicidal behaviors, gestures, threats, or self-harming behavior such as cutting?

7. Chronic Feelings of Emptiness: Do you frequently feel empty or bored, as if something is missing in your life?

8. Explosive Anger: Do you experience intense, inappropriate anger or have difficulty controlling your temper?

9. Feeling Disconnected: Have you felt paranoid or lost touch with reality, especially under stress?

This checklist is a steppingstone towards understanding your experiences or those of someone you care about. It highlights the need for empathy, support, and, most importantly, professional guidance in navigating the complexities of BPD. Remember, reaching out for help is a sign of strength and the first step towards healing.

Chapter Two
Diving Deeper

Nitin Pillai, a therapist at Spring Homeo, shares wisdom that lights the path for anyone touched by Borderline Personality Disorder (BPD). "It is essential to have accurate information on the common symptoms of BPD. Then, you can make a note of the points that cause emotional instability and explain your behavior correctly. In addition, learning about this condition develops empathy towards someone with BPD. It is always beneficial to get professional help from a mental health counselor or therapist. They will help you navigate through your feelings. Do not start a conversation when your partner is not ready. Instead, allow them to cool down and then strike up a conversation. Talking to them in a bad mood may worsen the situation. Try to learn the reasons for their sudden surge in emotions. Do not start a blame game and put the blame on a BPD patient. Instead, try to maintain your calm while talking to them. A sudden outburst in your emotions may make the situation more challenging. Always ask open-ended questions, as it makes a person feel heard. Moreover, do not force your opinion on them."

Pillai's advice underscores the heartbeat of this chapter: a deep dive into the complexities of BPD aimed at nurturing a rich understanding of its impact on individuals and their circles. With a spotlight on the defining features, symptoms, and broader implications, this chapter equips you with the knowledge to navigate the waters of BPD with grace. Understanding BPD is more than learning about a condition; it's about opening doors to effective communication, developing empathy, and building bridges of support. Through exploring the nuances of BPD, this chapter seeks to transform understanding into a powerful tool for connection, revealing the profound influence of empathy and informed conversation in managing life with BPD.

Key Features

Grasping the critical features of Borderline Personality Disorder is a crucial step toward unlocking its complexity. This understanding not only sheds light on the challenges faced by those with BPD but also fosters a more profound empathy and connection between them and their support networks. Let's embark on a detailed exploration of these defining characteristics to provide a clearer picture of the condition's impact on individuals and their relationships.

Emotional Instability and Interpersonal Relationships

Emotional instability refers to rapid changes in mood that can swing from joy to despair within moments, often without a clear cause. This condition can significantly affect one's sense of control and stability, similar to a clinical scenario where emotional responses fluctuate unpredictably, impacting daily functioning and relationships.

Interpersonal relationships for someone with BPD are equally turbulent. They may experience a profound fear of abandonment, clinging to relationships even when they sense a slight hint of separation. This fear can drive behaviors that appear contradictory—pushing loved ones away with intense reactions or demands, only to pull them back in, fearing isolation.

Relationships often fluctuate between idealization, where the other is seen as perfect, and devaluation, where they can do no right. Understanding these patterns is like decoding a complex dance, where deep-seated fears influence steps forward and back and the need for connection.

Symptoms and Implications

Beyond emotional instability and complex interpersonal relationships, a range of symptoms affect both personal and interpersonal spheres. Let's explore these features to understand their broader implications.

- Dysregulation: This refers to the difficulty in managing emotions, thoughts, and behaviors in a way that is considered normative. On a personal level, it can feel like an internal battle, with emotions flaring uncontrollably and thoughts racing unchecked. Interpersonally, it might lead to unpredictability, affecting relationships as others struggle to understand these swift changes.

- Anger and Impulsivity: Individuals with BPD may experience intense episodes of anger, sometimes erupting over seemingly minor triggers. This impulsivity can manifest in sudden decisions without considering the consequences, such as spending sprees or abrupt relationship changes. These moments can create waves in their social and professional lives, often leading to regret and misunderstanding among peers and loved ones.

- Sensitivity: Heightened sensitivity to emotional cues in the environment makes those with BPD exceptionally attuned to the feelings of others but also more susceptible to perceived criticism or rejection. While a strength in understanding and empathy, this sensitivity can also be a source of pain, as negative emotions are felt deeply and personally.

The interplay of these symptoms creates a complex landscape for individuals with BPD, challenging them to navigate a world that feels both intensely connected and painfully isolating. Recognizing these features illuminates the struggles faced and highlights the resilience and courage it takes to manage BPD daily.

Types of BPD

Borderline Personality Disorder, with its vast array of symptoms, manifests in diverse ways that can be categorized into four primary types. Understanding these can illuminate the varied experiences of those living with BPD, offering a more straightforward path to empathy and support.

- Discouraged BPD: Picture someone who often feels down, sees themselves in a negative light, and is overly dependent on others for their sense of worth. They may struggle with feelings of abandonment, leading them to cling to relationships. Despite their need for closeness, their fear might cause them to push others away, creating a cycle of dependency and rejection.

- Impulsive BPD: This type is characterized by a penchant for spur-of-the-moment decisions. Imagine a person who thrives on the thrill of new experiences but may not consider the long-term consequences of their actions. Their impulsivity can bring them into conflict with others and themselves as the aftermath of their choices becomes clear.

- Petulant BPD: Individuals with this type often oscillate between feelings of unworthiness and anger. They might quickly react with frustration or bitterness, especially when they feel misunderstood or neglected. Their emotional volatility can strain relationships as loved ones struggle to navigate their sudden mood shifts.

- Self-destructive BPD: Here, the person might engage in harmful behaviors, viewing themselves through a lens of self-loathing. They may sabotage their successes or relationships, driven by an inner belief that they don't deserve happiness. This self-destructive path is fraught with pitfalls.

Recognizing these types helps understand BPD's complexity and identify paths for intervention and support tailored to each individual's experiences.

Quiz: What's Your Type?

Take this quiz designed to shed light on the diverse manifestations of BPD. You might see which type resonates most with you by answering these questions. Remember, this quiz is for insight and understanding, not a diagnostic tool.

1. When faced with stress or conflict, you:

   - A) Feel deeply discouraged, preferring to lean on someone else for support.

   - B) Act on impulse, seeking immediate relief through action.

   - C) Quickly become irritable or angry, even over small matters.

   - D) Tend to engage in behaviors you know might harm you in the long run.

2. In relationships, you often feel:

- A) Clingy and fearful of being left alone.

- B) Excited but may move on quickly to new people or interests.

- C) Sensitive to signs of rejection, which can cause sudden anger.

- D) Unworthy of love, sometimes sabotaging relationships before they can leave you.

3. Your self-image:

- A) Is primarily negative, and you rely heavily on others' approval.

- B) Can change rapidly, mainly influenced by new experiences or challenges.

- C) Is often unstable, swinging between extremes based on the day or situation.

- D) Includes a harsh inner critic that leads to self-destructive choices.

Results:

- **Mostly A's:** Your answers align with the **Discouraged BPD** type. You may seek validation and fear abandonment, which can lead to dependency in relationships.

- **Mostly B's:** The **Impulsive BPD** type seems to fit. You're driven by the moment, which can make life exciting but sometimes leads to regrettable decisions.

- **Mostly C's:** Your responses suggest the **Petulant BPD** type. Emotional reactivity and unpredictability might characterize your relationships.

- **Mostly D's:** You might identify with the **Self-destructive BPD** type, engaging in harmful behaviors as a reflection of your self-view.

Understanding your type can open pathways to targeted strategies for managing BPD, enhancing your journey toward well-being.

Exercise: Mapping Your BPD Symptoms and Triggers

This exercise aims to help you map out your BPD symptoms alongside their triggers, offering a visual representation of your emotional landscape. By pinpointing what sparks your symptoms, you gain insight into managing your responses more effectively. Approach this task with an attitude of curiosity rather than criticism, allowing yourself to observe patterns without assigning blame.

Step 1: List Your Symptoms Start by listing your most frequent BPD symptoms. These might include episodes of intense anger, feelings of emptiness, impulsive actions, or rapid mood swings.

Step 2: Identify Your Triggers Next to each symptom, jot down specific situations, conversations, or thoughts that have historically led to these feelings or behaviors. Triggers can be as varied as a casual remark, a particular person's presence, or even a specific time of day.

Step 3: Create Your Map Draw lines connecting each symptom to its triggers, creating a visual map. This might reveal patterns or connections you hadn't noticed before, such as a particular trigger leading to multiple symptoms.

Step 4: Reflect and Plan With your map as a guide, consider strategies for addressing these triggers. This could involve setting boundaries in relationships, practicing mindfulness when encountering a known trigger, or preparing coping mechanisms in advance.

Remember, this map is not static. As you grow and change, your triggers and symptoms might too. Periodically revisiting and updating your map can provide ongoing insights into your journey with BPD, aiding in self-understanding and management.

Exercise: Complications Journal

Navigating Borderline Personality Disorder (BPD) often means contending with additional challenges. This exercise invites you to journal about these complexities, focusing on co-occurring issues such as anxiety, depression, or substance abuse. Through honest self-reflection, you can uncover patterns that may offer new insights into your coping strategies.

Journaling Prompts:

1. Identify Additional Challenges: What other mental health concerns or life challenges do you face alongside BPD? Describe how these interact with your BPD symptoms, creating an experience of your mental health.

2. Impact on Daily Life: How do these additional challenges affect your day-to-day activities, relationships, and your ability to manage BPD? Provide specific examples where the interplay between BPD and other issues became particularly evident.

3. Coping Strategies and Treatments: Reflect on any strategies or

treatments you have tried for these complications. What has helped? What hasn't? Consider both formal therapies and personal coping mechanisms.

4. Patterns and Insights: As you review your responses, do any patterns emerge? How might these insights enhance your perspective on your BPD and influence your strategies for addressing these challenges?

Approach this journaling exercise as an opportunity for deep exploration without judgment. The goal is to build a comprehensive understanding of your mental health landscape, recognizing the unique interconnections of BPD with other aspects of your life. This awareness can be a powerful tool in developing more effective coping strategies.

Reflection: How BPD Affects My Life and Relationships

Exploring the influence of BPD on your life offers a chance to acknowledge the challenges and recognize the resilience you've shown. This reflective exercise encourages you to examine the impact of BPD across various domains of your life, offering a structured way to consider both the struggles and the victories.

Family and Loved Ones:

- Reflect on how BPD has impacted your relationships with family members, such as parents or siblings. Have emotional intensity or fears of abandonment influenced these close bonds?

- Consider how your heightened sensitivity or empathy, traits often associated with BPD, have positively shaped these relationships. What supportive roles have your family members played, and how have they helped you manage your BPD?

Friendships:

- Reflect on how BPD has shaped your friendships. Are there moments where emotional intensity or fear of abandonment impacted these relationships?

- Consider times when your sensitivity or empathy, traits often heightened by BPD, enriched your friendships. How have you contributed positively to the lives of your friends?

Work:

- Think about the challenges BPD presents in the workplace, such as navigating interpersonal dynamics or managing stress.

- Identify moments of success at work, perhaps using your unique insights or adaptability to overcome obstacles or improve your environment.

Romantic Relationships:

- Examine the role of BPD in your romantic relationships. How have fears of abandonment or intensity of emotions played out?

- Reflect on the ways you've navigated these challenges to build meaningful connections, highlighting instances of growth and understanding.

Self-Worth:

- How has BPD affected your self-image and sense of worth? Are there specific triggers that tend to diminish your self-esteem?

- Acknowledge your resilience. Despite the struggles, what

strengths have you discovered in yourself? How have you shown courage and determination in your journey with BPD?

This reflective exercise is not just about acknowledging the impact of BPD but also about celebrating the resilience and strength you've shown in the face of these challenges.

Understanding BPD's complexity lays the groundwork for the crucial next steps—harnessing effective strategies for emotional regulation. The upcoming chapter transitions from insight to action, focusing on empowering you with the skills to navigate the emotional turbulence often experienced with BPD. Anticipate practical, actionable techniques designed to foster emotional stability, enhance interpersonal relationships, and improve overall well-being.

Chapter Three
Seeking Help

A recent study shines a beam of hope on the path to managing Borderline Personality Disorder: approximately 50% of individuals receiving treatment for BPD see significant improvement over a decade. This statistic isn't just a number; it's a testament to the power of professional help and the resilience of the human spirit. For those navigating the turbulent waters of BPD, these findings underscore a vital message: seeking help is not just a step but a leap toward recovery and a better quality of life.

Managing BPD requires consistent and professional intervention. Evidence-based treatments and support systems are crucial, providing the necessary tools and guidance for individuals to effectively manage their symptoms. The effectiveness of seeking help goes beyond alleviating symptoms; it's about reclaiming one's life from the shadows of BPD. This chapter explains why professional guidance, self-help strategies, and the support of loved ones are not just options but essential components of a comprehensive management plan for BPD. Each step towards seeking help is a progressive move from challenge to recovery, significantly impacting the individual's quality of life.

The Importance of Seeking Help

Taking the step to seek help marks a pivotal moment in the journey towards recovery. It's a proactive decision acknowledging the need for change and the desire for a better quality of life. This move towards finding support and treatment is crucial, acting as the foundation upon which recovery is built. It's a sign of strength, a commitment to self-improvement, and an act of hope for a future where managing BPD becomes a reality.

Professional Help and Treatment Options

The journey towards wellness often begins in the quiet confines of a therapist's office, where the chaos of BPD finds understanding and strategies for management. Among the myriad of treatment options, psychotherapy emerges as a beacon of hope by offering tailored pathways to recovery. Such approaches include Dialectical Behavior Therapy (DBT), Mentalization-Based Treatment (MBT), and Schema Therapy, each designed to address the specific needs of individuals with BPD.

Dialectical Behavior Therapy (DBT) focuses on equipping individuals with skills to manage emotional distress, improve interpersonal relationships, and cultivate mindfulness. Imagine finding calm in the storm of overwhelming emotions by learning to navigate your feelings with grace and resilience.

Mentalization-Based Treatment (MBT) invites individuals to a deeper understanding of themselves and others by enhancing their ability to interpret and reflect on their own and others' mental states. This method focuses on developing one's capacity for "mentalizing," which is understanding the thoughts, feelings, and intentions behind one's and others' behaviors. This is particularly crucial in maintaining relationships and managing emotions effectively.

Schema Therapy delves into the roots of BPD, addressing lifelong patterns and deeply ingrained beliefs that fuel the disorder. Through this therapy, envision rewriting your story, transforming harmful schemas into narratives of strength and recovery.

Alongside these therapies, building a support network emerges as equally vital. Support groups, whether in-person or online, serve as sanctuaries where shared experiences weave a fabric of communal resilience. Here, individuals are reminded they are not alone in their struggles; instead, they find strength in numbers, drawing courage from others' journeys towards healing.

The tapestry of treatment options and the solidarity of a support network underscore a powerful message: recovery is not a solitary endeavor. It's a journey made more affluent and more attainable through the collective strength of professional guidance and community support.

Exercise: Safety Plan

Creating a personalized safety plan is a proactive measure for anyone managing the unpredictable Borderline Personality Disorder. This plan acts as a lifeline, a concrete strategy to manage moments of crisis or intense emotional turmoil. By evaluating behaviors, identifying triggers, and documenting coping resources, you can craft a plan that safeguards your well-being and empowers you to take control of your journey toward recovery.

Step 1: Evaluate Your Behaviors Begin by reflecting on your behaviors, particularly those that emerge during times of distress. Recognize patterns or actions that may escalate situations or contribute to emotional upheaval. This introspection is not about self-judgment but about understanding and awareness.

Step 2: Identify Your Triggers Next, pinpoint the triggers that catalyze your challenging behaviors or emotional responses. These triggers may include various elements, from specific individuals and particular scenarios to distinct times of the day. By recognizing these triggers, you establish the foundation for your safety plan, equipping yourself with knowledge on what to anticipate and prepare for.

Step 3: Document Your Coping Resources With a clear view of your behaviors and triggers, list coping mechanisms that have proven helpful in the past or new strategies you wish to try. These resources could include breathing exercises, contacting a trusted friend, or engaging in a grounding activity.

Step 4: Make a Safety Plan Commitment Finally, commit to your safety plan. Document it in a way that resonates with you, whether digitally or on paper. Consider sharing this plan with someone you trust, making it a shared commitment to your well-being.

By taking these steps, you acknowledge BPD's challenges and actively equip yourself with tools to navigate them. Your safety plan is a testament to your resilience and determination, a customized guide tailored to your unique path toward stability and health.

Exercise: Support System Mapping

Building and recognizing your support system is a critical component. This exercise aims to help you visually map out the network of support around you, encouraging you to identify both existing pillars and potential new sources of support.

Step 1: Identify Your Current Support System Begin by listing the individuals who currently form your support network. These can include family members, friends, healthcare professionals, or even colleagues who offer understanding, assistance, or a listening ear. On a piece of paper or a digital document, write down their names and the specific kind of support they provide. This process not only helps you see the wealth of support available but also allows you to appreciate the diverse roles people play in your journey.

Step 2: Explore Additional Support Options Next, consider expanding your support system by joining BPD support groups or engaging with online communities. These groups offer a unique space where shared experiences foster a deep sense of understanding and empathy. To start, research local or online BPD support groups, focusing on those that resonate with your needs and preferences.

Step 3: Engage Actively with Support Groups Upon joining a group, aim to participate actively. Share your experiences, listen attentively to others, and practice empathy. Engaging with these communities can significantly enhance your sense of belonging and provide practical strategies for coping with BPD.

Benefits of Support Groups Support groups bring the invaluable benefit of shared understanding. They offer a platform for exchanging coping mechanisms, reducing feelings of isolation, and building connections with others who truly understand the challenges of living with BPD. By mapping out your support system and actively engaging in support groups, you solidify a network of resources that can buoy you through the ebbs and flows of managing BPD.

For Families: Finding a BPD Family Support Group

These groups offer a sanctuary where families can share experiences, gain insights, and find comfort in knowing they are not alone. The journey with

BPD affects not just the individual but also permeates the entire family dynamic, making a collective support network essential.

To find a BPD family support group, start with online research or consult mental health professionals who can direct you to local or virtual resources. Websites dedicated to mental health and BPD often list support groups, providing details on their focus, meeting times, and how to join. Please don't overlook the power of social media platforms and forums, where many support groups advertise their meetings and share valuable content.

Engaging with a family support group brings multiple benefits, including understanding the disorder from new perspectives, learning effective communication strategies, and fostering a supportive environment at home. These groups empower families to navigate the challenges of BPD with resilience, ensuring that no one feels isolated in their experience.

Having established the bedrock of support through professional help and community, we pivot to mastering emotional regulation skills in the next chapter. This transition marks a crucial phase in the journey, where learning to navigate the emotional waves of BPD with skill and grace becomes our focus, setting the stage for transformative growth and recovery.

Chapter Four
Emotional Regulation Skills

Effective emotional regulation can transform lives, particularly for those managing Borderline Personality Disorder. Research confirms that mastering this skill soothes the daily ups and downs and significantly improves relationships and overall happiness. Imagine the power of maintaining calm during a heated conversation or feeling a surge of joy without fear of it plummeting to despair.

In this chapter, you will discover techniques to gain control over your emotions and experience them in a healthier and more balanced manner. Rather than merely suppressing negative feelings, we will explore creating a space where all emotions can coexist without overwhelming you. This balance is essential for not just surviving but also thriving with BPD.

The Importance of Emotional Regulation

Emotional regulation involves managing and responding to intense feelings in a way that is socially acceptable and beneficial. For individuals with Borderline Personality Disorder, this skill is vital. Their emotional responses can be unpredictable and extreme, leading to severe consequences in personal relationships and daily functioning. Mastering emotional regulation helps stabilize these responses, allowing for more meaningful interactions and a greater sense of control over their lives. This section outlines key strategies to cultivate this essential skill, setting the stage for improved well-being. Let's explore how to build this crucial skill.

The Benefits of Emotional Regulation

Developing solid emotional regulation skills offers profound benefits. It enhances your ability to relate to others, stabilizes your mood, and increases overall happiness. By implementing the strategies outlined in this chapter, you will build the foundation for a more fulfilling and emotionally stable life.

Enhanced Problem-Solving Abilities

When unchecked, emotions can cloud judgment and hinder the ability to think critically. Effective emotional regulation clears the mind, enabling sharper decision-making and problem-solving skills. Research highlights that with improved emotional control, individuals with BPD are better equipped to assess situations logically and make informed decisions, reducing impulsivity and poor judgment often seen in high-stress scenarios.

Stress Reduction

High emotional reactivity is a hallmark of BPD, often leading to overwhelming stress. Learning to regulate emotional responses can significantly lower daily stress levels. Techniques that focus on managing physiological reactions to stress, like deep breathing and mindfulness, prove to be effective. A study from API Behavioral Health Services underscores the importance of emotional regulation in reducing overall stress, showing that individuals who practice these skills can better handle life's pressures and recover more quickly from setbacks.

Improved Relationships

Perhaps one of the most significant impacts of effective emotional regulation is on personal relationships. BPD can make relationships volatile, but with better control over emotions, individuals report more stable and satisfying interactions with others. The ability to remain calm during emotional exchanges helps prevent conflicts and deepens connections. Medical News Today supports this, explaining how emotional regulation fosters empathy and understanding, which are both crucial components for healthy relationships.

By integrating these emotional regulation strategies, individuals with BPD enhance their competence and resilience and improve their interactions and overall quality of life. The evidence is clear: managing emotions effectively lays the groundwork for a more stable and fulfilling existence.

Exercise: Deep Breathing

Deep breathing is not just a way to relax; it's a powerful tool for emotional regulation. By consciously controlling your breathing, you can directly influence your emotional state, helping to calm intense emotions and stabilize mood swings commonly experienced by individuals with Borderline Personality Disorder. This section provides detailed step-by-step instructions for several deep breathing techniques, each designed to enhance emotional regulation.

Technique 1: The 4-7-8 Breath

Developed by Dr. Andrew Weil, the 4-7-8 breathing technique is simple yet effective in reducing anxiety and bringing about a state of calm. It's beneficial when feelings of stress and tension rise.

1. Exhale completely through your mouth, making a whoosh sound.

2. Close your mouth and inhale quietly through your nose to a mental count of four.

3. Hold your breath for a count of seven.

4. Exhale completely through your mouth, making a whoosh sound to a count of eight.

5. This is one breath. Now, inhale again and repeat the cycle three more times for a total of four breaths.

Technique 2: Diaphragmatic Breathing

Also known as belly breathing, this technique focuses on fully engaging the diaphragm during breathing, which is vital for maximum oxygen exchange and has a direct impact on calming the parasympathetic nervous system.

1. Lie on your back on a flat surface or in bed, with your knees bent and your head supported. You can use a pillow under your knees to support your legs.

2. Place one hand on your upper chest and the other just below your rib cage. This will allow you to feel your diaphragm move as you breathe.

3. Breathe in slowly through your nose so that your stomach moves out against your hand. The hand on your chest should remain as still as possible.

4. Tighten your stomach muscles, letting them fall inward as you exhale through pursed lips. The hand on your stomach should move in as you exhale, but your other hand should move very little.

5. Practice this technique for 5 to 10 minutes 3 to 4 times daily.

Technique 3: Alternate Nostril Breathing

This yoga breathing practice is called Nadi Shodhana. It is believed to balance the body and calm the mind.

1. Sit in a comfortable position with your legs crossed.

2. Place your left hand on your left knee. Using the thumb of your right hand, close your right nostril.

3. Inhale slowly through your left nostril.

4. Using the ring finger of your right hand, close your left nostril, release the thumb from the right nostril, and exhale slowly through the right nostril.

5. Inhale through the right nostril, **close it, then exhale through the left nostril.**

6. Continue this alternating pattern **for several cycles, focusing on your breath.**

Each of these techniques is a practical method to control and reduce the intensity of emotional responses. Incorporating these breathing exercises into your daily routine can significantly improve emotional regulation and serve as immediate tools for those moments when emotions begin to feel overwhelming. Regular practice can make a profound difference in managing the symptoms of Borderline Personality Disorder and enhancing overall emotional stability.

Exercise: Positive Self-Talk

Positive self-talk is a fundamental technique in the toolkit for managing emotions. This form of internal dialogue can shift your mindset from critical and negative to empowering and affirmative.

Adopting a habit of positive self-talk can significantly enhance your mental health and improve your relationships. This approach helps mitigate stress and anxiety, boosts self-esteem, and supports attaining personal goals. In your interactions with others it cultivates a compassionate and empathetic stance, which is essential for nurturing healthy relationships.

Comparing Negative and Positive Self-Talk

Practice Worksheet: Shifting to Positive Self-Talk

To help you cultivate a habit of positive self-talk, follow this simple worksheet approach:

IDENTIFY - CHALLENGE - REFRAME - REFLECT

1. Identify Negative Thoughts: Throughout the day, jot down any negative thoughts that come to mind.

2. Challenge These Thoughts: For each negative thought, ask yourself:

   - Is this thought based on facts or my emotions?

   - Is there evidence to support this thought?

   - How would I respond if a friend said this about themselves?

3. Reframe the Thought: Convert each negative thought into a positive one using the table above as a guide.

4. Reflect on the Outcome: At the end of the week, reflect on how changing your thoughts has affected your feelings and behaviors.

This practice trains you to reframe negative thoughts automatically and helps you become more mindful of the tone and content of your internal dialogue.

Continuing Your Practice

To effectively integrate positive self-talk into your daily routine, consider setting reminders that prompt you to pause and reflect on your thought patterns. You might use smartphone alarms, apps designed for habit-building, or even sticky notes placed in visible locations as practical tools for these reminders. Gradually, this technique will become a natural part of your mental processing, leading to enduring changes in how you perceive and react to the world around you. Enhanced emotional regulation and relationship skills are just a few of the benefits you will notice as you make positive self-talk a habit.

Exercise: What are My Hobbies?

Hobbies play a crucial role in enhancing mental health by providing a meaningful escape from the stress of daily life. They offer a unique opportunity to engage in activities that bring joy, reduce stress, and connect with others, which are vital components to building a balanced lifestyle.

Boosting Mental Health Through Hobbies

Engaging in hobbies can significantly lessen feelings of depression and anxiety. Activities that capture your attention and imagination can act as natural distractions, helping you break free from negative thought patterns. They also promote a sense of accomplishment and pride, boosting your self-esteem and overall mood. Whether it's crafting, gardening, or learning a new musical instrument, hobbies provide a therapeutic benefit by allowing you to express yourself in non-verbal ways, which is particularly useful for those who find verbal expression challenging.

Exploring New Hobbies

Finding the right hobby can be a journey of self-discovery. Here are a variety of hobbies to consider, tailored to different interests and abilities:

- Creative Arts: Painting, drawing, pottery, or writing can be soothing and provide a tangible output for your emotions.

- Physical Activities: Walking, group exercise classes, yoga, or hiking not only keeps you fit but also improves your mental health by releasing endorphins.

- Learning and Education: Explore a new language or enroll in courses about history, science, or artificial intelligence to keep your mind engaged and challenged.

- Music and Dance: Learn to play an instrument, take dance lessons, or a Zumba class. These activities are great for emotional expression and can also be social.

- Gardening: Connect with nature and enjoy the satisfaction of growing your own food or beautifying your surroundings with plants.

- Volunteering: Find a cause you are passionate about and contribute your time. Helping others can improve your mood, give you satisfaction, and broaden your social network.

Integrating Hobbies into Your Life

To fully benefit from hobbies, it's essential to integrate them into your routine:

1. Create Goals: Setting small, achievable goals within your hobby can motivate you and give you something to look forward to.

2. Set Specific Times: Dedicate regular time slots each week for your hobbies to ensure you consistently engage in them.

3. Join Groups: For social hobbies, joining clubs or special interest groups can enhance your experience and provide social support.

4. Celebrate Progress: Take time to acknowledge your improvements or achievements within your hobby to boost your confidence and motivation.

Hobbies are not just pastimes; they are essential tools for mental health management, providing joy, fulfillment, and a sense of belonging. As you delve into these activities, you'll discover that they enrich your life and contribute to a healthier, more balanced mental state.

Daily Journal

Keeping a daily journal is a powerful tool for anyone, particularly for those navigating the emotional waves of Borderline Personality Disorder. This practice helps track emotions and serves as a reflective process that can foster greater self-awareness and emotional regulation.

Setting Up Your Journaling Habit

To start, invest in a journal that feels personal and inviting—whether a simple notebook, a digital app, or a beautifully bound book. Decide on a specific time each day for journaling, ideally when you can have a quiet moment by yourself. This could be first thing in the morning, during a lunch break, or just before bedtime. Consistency is key, so aim to make journaling a fixed part of your daily routine.

Journaling Prompts to Guide Your Entries

To get the most out of your journaling, use prompts that encourage you to explore your emotions and reactions in depth. Here are some prompts to get you started:

1. My Emotions Today: Describe the emotions you felt today. Were

there any triggers? How did you respond to them?

2. Gratitude List: Write down three things you are grateful for today and why. Reflect on how acknowledging these can affect your mood.

3. Challenging Interactions: Reflect on any problematic interactions. What emotions arose? How might you handle a similar situation differently in the future?

4. Accomplishments: Note any achievements of the day, no matter how small. How did you contribute to these successes?

5. Future Self: Write a letter to your future self about your hopes or where you see yourself overcoming current challenges.

6. **Positive Self-Talk Practice:** Did you practice positive self-talk today? List one positive affirmation you used.

7. **Mood Improvement Actions:** Did you do something today to improve your mood?

8. **Personal Time:** Did you take time for yourself today? Describe what you did and how it made you feel.

Maintaining Your Journaling Practice

To keep your journaling habit strong, regularly review your past entries. This review process can illuminate patterns in your emotional responses and highlight areas of improvement or growth. It can also be gratifying to see how far you have come in managing your emotions and reactions.

Encourage yourself to be honest in your entries. The more truthful you are with your journal, the more insight you'll gain from the process.

Remember, this journal is a private space to express yourself freely—there is no right or wrong way to fill its pages.

By committing to this simple yet effective tool, you gain a clearer picture of your emotional landscape and equip yourself with the knowledge to navigate it more skillfully. Journaling is not just about recording events—it's about discovering and owning your narrative.

Brief Guide: Mindfulness and Its Benefits for BPD

Mindfulness is a practice rooted in being fully present and engaged in the moment, aware of your thoughts and feelings without judgment. For individuals with Borderline Personality Disorder, mindfulness offers a path to manage their emotional turbulence better and enhance their daily interactions.

Understanding Mindfulness

At its core, mindfulness involves a deliberate focus on one's current experience, cultivating a heightened awareness that can diffuse the intensity of emotional responses typical in BPD. By practicing mindfulness, you can develop the ability to observe your feelings and thoughts without becoming overwhelmed by them, thereby reducing impulsive reactions and fostering a greater sense of calm.

Benefits of Mindfulness for BPD

The benefits of mindfulness for those with BPD are well-documented. It enhances emotional regulation, decreases reactivity to stress, and improves overall mental clarity. Studies have shown that mindfulness training can lead to significant reductions in the symptoms of anxiety, depression, and stress, all of which are common among individuals with BPD. By helping to break the cycle of negative thought patterns, mindfulness facilitates a more balanced perspective and improves relational interactions.

Simple Mindfulness Exercises

Here are a few basic mindfulness exercises designed to be accessible and immediately beneficial:

1. Mindful Breathing: Focus solely on your breath entering and leaving your body. Observe the sensation of breathing without attempting to change it. This can be done for just a minute or two and is especially useful during moments of high stress.

2. Mindful Observation: Choose an object from your surroundings and focus on observing it for a minute or two. Notice the color, shape, texture, and any other qualities without any judgment. This practice helps bring your attention back to the present moment.

3. Body Scan: Whether lying down or sitting in a chair, find a comfortable position and slowly bring your attention to each part of your body, from your toes to your head. Notice any sensations, tension, or discomfort. This practice can help you connect your physical sensations with your emotional state, making it suitable for any setting, including at work.

Activity: Guided Mindfulness Practices

Mindfulness can be a sanctuary for those battling the emotional storms of Borderline Personality Disorder. The following guided practices are designed to be straightforward and adaptable, allowing you to incorporate mindfulness into your daily life, no matter where you are or what you're doing.

1. Five Senses Exercise 5-4-3-2-1

This quick exercise helps you ground yourself in the present and can be particularly helpful during moments of distress or overwhelm.

- See: Identify five things you can see around you. It could be a small detail like a pattern on the carpet or something broader like the way light plays on the wall.

- Touch: Notice four things you can touch. Feel the texture of your clothing, the surface of the table, or the coolness of a glass.

- Hear: Listen for three sounds. It might be the hum of traffic, birds chirping, or someone's distant laughter.

- Smell: Detect two things you can smell. Maybe you catch the aroma of coffee or the scent of a flower.

- Taste: Focus on one thing you can taste. This could be the lingering taste of a meal or even the freshness of water.

2. Mindful Walking

Turn a regular walk into a rejuvenating mindfulness practice by focusing on the experience of walking.

- As you walk, pay attention to the sensation of your feet touching the ground with each step.

- Notice the rhythm of your walk and the movement of your arms.

- Take in the sights around you, experiencing each visual moment as you move through it.

- Listen to the sounds around you, fully experiencing each auditory moment.

3. Two-Minute Breathing Space

This practice is perfect for those who need a quick way to center themselves, maybe on a hectic day or when needed.

- Sit or stand in a comfortable position and close your eyes.

- Spend a full minute focusing solely on your breath, observing its natural flow without trying to change it.

- For the next minute or so, maintain a gentle focus on your breath, slowly open your eyes, and expand your awareness to include your body and the environment around you, maintaining a gentle focus on your breath.

Each of these activities is designed to anchor you firmly in the present, helping to alleviate anxiety and stress. By practicing these simple exercises, you can cultivate a more mindful approach to your day.

Activity: Relaxation Technique and Reflection

Relaxation techniques are essential tools for managing stress and reducing the intensity of emotional responses, especially for individuals coping with Borderline Personality Disorder. This section will guide you through progressive muscle relaxation and visualization, two effective methods for calming the mind and body. After each exercise, you'll be encouraged to reflect on your emotional state, helping to deepen your understanding of how relaxation impacts your feelings.

Progressive Muscle Relaxation (PMR)

Progressive muscle relaxation involves tensing and then relaxing different muscle groups in the body, which can help relieve physical and emotional tension.

1. Find a Comfortable Position: Sit or lie down in a quiet place where you won't be disturbed.

2. Tense and Relax Your Muscle: Begin with your feet. Tense them for 5-10 seconds and then relax for 20-30 seconds, paying attention to the sensation of release. Continue this process sequentially for each muscle group: move up to your calves, then thighs, hands, arms, stomach, chest, shoulders, and eyes. You will find the amount of time that works best for you.

3. Breathe Deeply: As you relax your muscles, focus on your breathing. Inhale deeply through your nose, hold for a few seconds, and exhale slowly through your mouth.

4. Move Slowly: After completing the exercise, take a few minutes to sit or lie quietly. Allow your body to relax completely.

Visualization

Visualization, or guided imagery, involves forming mental images to take a visual journey through a peaceful scene or a desired outcome.

1. Choose Your Setting: Find a quiet place and close your eyes. Imagine a place where you feel calm and safe. This could be a beach, a forest, or a cozy room.

2. Engage Your Senses: Visualize the details of this place. What do you see? What sounds do you hear? Can you smell anything? For example, if you're on a beach, imagine the sound of waves, the smell of saltwater, and the warmth of the sun on your skin.

3. Deepen the Experience: Spend several minutes in your peaceful place. With each breath, allow yourself to become more relaxed

and immersed in the environment.

4. Return Gradually: When you're ready, slowly bring your awareness back to your current setting. Open your eyes and take a moment to adjust.

Reflective Exercise

After completing each relaxation technique, take a few minutes to reflect on your emotional state.

- Note Your Feelings: How did you feel before and after the exercise? Were there any changes in your level of stress or anxiety?

- Record Your Observations: Keep a journal of these reflections. Note any patterns or changes over time. This can help you understand which techniques work best for you and how your emotional responses evolve with practice.

Regularly practicing these relaxation techniques and reflecting on your experiences will give you valuable insights into your emotional well-being and develop more effective ways to manage your emotions. This proactive approach can lead to significant improvements in your overall mental health and quality of life.

As we have explored various methods to manage emotions and cultivate a calmer mind, we must recognize that emotional well-being is deeply intertwined with physical health. The next chapter will delve into how maintaining physical health can significantly enhance emotional stability. We'll explore practical steps to integrate physical health strategies that support and amplify the emotional regulation skills developed in this chapter. Together, these elements form a comprehensive approach to managing

BPD, highlighting the vital connection between a healthy body and a healthy mind.

Chapter Five
Physical Health

Research shows that individuals with Borderline Personality Disorder face a higher risk of various physical health issues, including serious chronic diseases like diabetes, heart disease, and arthritis. This striking fact underscores the critical need for a holistic approach to wellness that prioritizes both mental and physical health. In BPD, the mind and body are intricately linked, with each significantly impacting the other. Therefore, enhancing physical health is not just about preventing or managing illness; it's about creating a foundation that supports emotional regulation and overall quality of life. This chapter delves into the vital connection between your physical well-being and your mental health, offering practical strategies to strengthen both. By understanding and addressing the physical aspects of your health, you can better manage the emotional challenges of BPD, leading to a more balanced and fulfilling life.

The Connection Between Physical Health and BPD

The relationship between physical health and Borderline Personality Disorder is bidirectional; each profoundly influences the other. Physical ailments often exacerbate the psychological distress associated with BPD. At the same time, the emotional turbulence characteristic of BPD can lead to physical health declines, creating a cycle that can challenge the management of both. Addressing this interconnectedness is crucial, as it opens pathways to more effective treatments and improved quality of life, demonstrating that wellness is not just a state of the body or the mind but both in unison.

Detailed Discussion

The physical health risks linked with Borderline Personality Disorder extend beyond psychological distress, manifesting significantly in increased susceptibility to chronic diseases. Research published in the Journal of Clinical Psychiatry reveals that the erratic lifestyle habits associated with BPD—stemming from impulsivity and emotional instability—often lead to detrimental physical health outcomes, such as diabetes and heart disease.

"Individuals with BPD have a heightened risk of chronic physical conditions, which compounds their psychological burden and complicates treatment," states the study. This link is particularly evident with diabetes and cardiovascular diseases, where the prevalence rates among those with BPD are alarmingly higher than in the general population. These conditions are exacerbated by common BPD-related behaviors, including poor dietary choices, inadequate physical activity, and substance abuse, which all contribute to the deterioration of physical health.

Managing these physical health issues is shown to have a reciprocal benefit on the symptoms of BPD. According to the research, interventions that focus on lifestyle modifications—such as improved nutrition, regular exercise, and better sleep habits—address the direct risk factors for chronic diseases, enhance emotional regulation, and reduce stress. This holistic management approach is crucial, as it underscores the interconnectedness of physical and mental health in individuals with BPD.

"The bidirectional relationship between chronic physical illnesses and the severity of BPD symptoms suggests that comprehensive care should integrate both physical and mental health treatments," the study concludes. By adopting such integrated strategies, individuals with BPD can achieve better overall health outcomes, illustrating the critical need for health care frameworks that encompass a full spectrum of care for this complex disorder.

Importance of Physical Health Practices

For individuals with Borderline Personality Disorder, engaging in specific physical health practices is not just beneficial; it's transformative. These essential activities include regular physical exercise, maintaining a balanced diet, and ensuring consistent, quality sleep. Each of these practices plays a pivotal role in enhancing both physical and mental health, helping to stabilize mood fluctuations and reduce stress levels.

Physical Activity, Sleep, and Diet

Physical Activity

Regular exercise has been shown to alleviate symptoms of depression and anxiety, common comorbidities in BPD. According to research, engaging in moderate aerobic exercise at least three times a week can enhance mood stability by releasing endorphins, often referred to as feel-good hormones. For those new to exercise, starting with brisk walking or gentle yoga sessions can be a practical and enjoyable way to integrate physical activity into daily life without feeling overwhelmed.

Sleep

Quality sleep is crucial for emotional regulation and mental clarity. Disturbed sleep patterns can exacerbate the emotional volatility associated with BPD. To improve sleep hygiene, it is recommended to establish a consistent bedtime routine, limit exposure to screens before bedtime, and create a restful environment—dark, cool, and quiet. The National Institutes of Health highlights the importance of sleep-in reducing BPD-related impairments, suggesting that 7-9 hours of sleep per night can markedly improve daily functioning.

Food

A balanced diet plays a pivotal role in managing BPD by influencing mood and energy levels. Nutritional psychiatry research underscores the benefits of a diet rich in vegetables, fruits, lean proteins, and whole grains while advising minimization of processed foods and sugar, which can lead to mood swings. Implementing structured mealtimes and planning balanced meals can help individuals with BPD maintain stable blood sugar levels, which is crucial for emotional stability.

By adopting these healthful practices, individuals with BPD can experience not only a reduction in symptoms but also an overall enhancement in quality of life. These changes, while seemingly simple, require consistency and commitment, yet the benefits they bring can be life-altering.

Activities:

Wellness Journal

To effectively manage both physical and emotional health, it's essential for individuals with Borderline Personality Disorder to monitor their wellness activities and observe how this impacts their mental state. This section introduces practical tools and guidelines designed to help you track your daily health behaviors and their effects on your emotional well-being.

Physical Activity Log

Documenting your exercise routines can motivate you to stay consistent and can also illustrate the correlation between physical activity and mood improvement. Over time, this log will highlight the positive impacts of regular exercise on your mental health, reinforcing the habit. Include:

- Type of Exercise: What activity did you do?

- Duration: How long did you exercise?

- Intensity: Was it light, moderate, or intense?

- Pre- and Post-Exercise Mood: How did you feel before and after? This log can be maintained in a digital spreadsheet or a dedicated fitness app that allows for notetaking.

Sleep Diary

Keeping a sleep diary can provide insights into how sleep patterns affect mood and emotional regulation. A sleep diary helps you record and analyze patterns that affect your sleep quality and duration, which is crucial for mental health. Here's what to track:

- Time: When did you go to bed and wake up?

- Quality: Rate your sleep quality on a scale of 1 to 10.

- Interruptions: Did anything wake you up? How long were you awake?

- Daytime Sleepiness: Note any instances of feeling unusually tired or needing to nap.

- Mood: Record your mood upon waking and throughout the day. You can create a simple table in a notebook or use a digital app designed to track your sleep and mood.

Food Diary

Keeping track of your dietary habits helps identify how your eating affects your emotional state. Detail your meals, eating times, and any mood changes throughout the day. This information is valuable for pinpointing foods that boost your energy and mood stability or trigger adverse reactions. Track:

- Meals and Snacks: What did you eat and when?

- Portions: How much did you consume?

- Mood: How did you feel after eating?

- Physical Reactions: Any physical discomfort or energy changes? Use a notebook or a diet tracking app to keep this diary, making sure to update it regularly throughout the day.

Using the Wellness Journal

These tools—Sleep Diary, Physical Activity Log, and Food Diary—are integral to managing your health. They allow you and your healthcare provider to analyze the interactions between your lifestyle choices and mental health, forming a comprehensive strategy for managing BPD symptoms.

With a strong focus on physical health management, we now transition to another vital aspect of living with BPD: navigating relationships. The skills and habits developed in this chapter contribute significantly to emotional stability, which is crucial for managing complex interpersonal dynamics. The next chapter will delve into strategies for building and maintaining healthy relationships that support both personal growth and emotional well-being.

Chapter Six
Navigating Relationships

Interpersonal relationships can either be a source of immense joy or profound stress, particularly for individuals with Borderline Personality Disorder. The intense emotions and fears characteristic of BPD, such as the fear of abandonment or episodes of intense anger, often complicate personal and professional interactions. This chapter explores the intricate dynamics of relationships through the lens of BPD and provides targeted strategies and tools designed to foster understanding, enhance communication, and improve overall relationship health.

For those managing BPD, navigating the complexities of relationships is not merely about maintaining connections but about transforming them into sources of support and stability. This chapter aims to empower individuals with BPD to steer their interpersonal engagements toward more positive outcomes by delving into the roots of common relationship challenges and introducing practical exercises and techniques. As we unfold the layers of relationship dynamics, we equip you with the knowledge and skills to manage and improve these critical aspects of your life, paving the way for more meaningful and enduring connections.

Relationship Challenges with BPD

Borderline Personality Disorder introduces distinctive hurdles in relationships, marked by emotional volatility and an intense fear of abandonment. These core challenges often manifest as instability within interpersonal connections, where individuals with BPD might experience rapid shifts in feelings and attitudes toward others.

This instability can strain relationships, creating cycles of intense closeness followed by sudden withdrawal. The fear of being left alone can lead to behaviors that paradoxically push others away, complicating efforts to maintain healthy and stable relationships. Understanding these dynamics is crucial for managing BPD in the context of personal interactions.

Detailing Specific Challenges

Borderline Personality Disorder significantly colors the way individuals perceive and interact within relationships. Beyond emotional instability and fears of abandonment, specific behaviors like impulsivity and dishonesty frequently emerge, complicating connections with friends, family, and colleagues.

Impulsive Behaviors

Impulsivity in BPD can manifest as sudden decisions that disrupt relationship stability—like abruptly ending relationships, moving, or changing jobs without warning. These actions often stem from intense emotional moments rather than careful thought, leading to regret and damage to relationships that may be difficult to repair. This impulsiveness can also extend to spending, substance use, or sexual relationships, further destabilizing the person's life and affecting their loved ones.

According to Healthline, these actions are attempts to manage overwhelming feelings and stress but typically backfire, undermining trust and security in relationships.

Lying

Dishonesty can be another challenge in relationships affected by BPD. As noted by Verywell Mind-https://www.verywellmind.com, individuals with BPD might use lying as a tool to cope with feelings of inadequacy or to avoid perceived threats of abandonment. For example, they may exaggerate personal achievements or fabricate stories about interactions with others. These falsehoods, although often meant to protect their relationships or self-esteem, usually create significant conflict and mistrust among those close to them.

Understanding and Mitigation

Recognizing these behaviors as part of the disorder is crucial for both the individual with BPD and their loved ones. Effective communication strategies, like those discussed in Verywell Health-https://www.verywell mind.com, encourage open and honest dialogue that addresses behaviors non-confrontationally. By focusing on expressing feelings and needs without judgment, individuals can break the cycle of impulsive actions and dishonesty, paving the way for healthier interactions.

Addressing these specific challenges requires patience, understanding, and often professional guidance to develop healthier relational patterns for everyone involved.

Exercise: Understanding Your Attachment Style

Understanding your attachment style can profoundly impact how you navigate relationships, providing critical insights into your interaction patterns. Attachment styles, developed early in life, influence how individuals relate to others emotionally and can play a significant role in the dynamics of their relationships. This exercise introduces a quiz designed to help you identify your attachment style, offering a clearer understanding of how it affects your interpersonal connections.

Attachment Styles Overview

- Secure Attachment: Individuals with a secure attachment style tend to have healthy, stable relationships. They feel comfortable with intimacy and are usually warm and loving.

- Anxious Attachment: Those with an anxious attachment style often worry about the stability of their relationships. They seek closeness and assurance but may act clingy or overly dependent on others.

- Avoidant Attachment: People with an avoidant attachment style value their independence above all. They might appear distant and may struggle with intimacy, often pulling away when things get too close.

- Disorganized Attachment: This style is a mix of anxious and avoidant traits. Individuals with disorganized attachment might find it hard to trust others and often show mixed signals, craving closeness but fearing it at the same time.

Quiz: Discover Your Attachment Style

1. How do you react when someone gets too close in a relationship?

A. I feel comfortable and happy.

B. I get nervous and worry they might leave.

C. I start feeling the need for space.

D.I'm confused, wanting closeness but feeling uncomfortable.

1. What is your biggest fear in a relationship?

A. I don't have significant fears about relationships.

B. That my partner will leave me.

C. Losing my independence.

D. That I can't trust my partner.

1. How do you handle conflicts in relationships?

A. I try to resolve them through communication.

B. I worry conflicts could end the relationship.

C. I withdraw or prefer not to address conflicts.

D. I find conflicts unsettling and react unpredictably.

Interpreting Your Answers:

- Mostly A's: Your responses lean towards a Secure attachment style.

- Mostly B's: Your answers suggest an Anxious attachment style.

- Mostly C's: You might have an Avoidant attachment style.

- Mostly D's: It appears you have a Disorganized attachment style.

By understanding your attachment style, you can begin to work on areas that may need improvement and leverage your strengths in forming and maintaining healthy relationships. This awareness is crucial in both personal growth and the development of fulfilling connections with others.

Exercise: Relationship Mapping

Mapping your relationships provides a visual representation of your current connections, illuminating how symptoms of Borderline Personality Disorder might influence these interactions. This exercise aims to help you identify recurring patterns or themes within your relationships, offering insights into the dynamics shaped by BPD.

Step-by-Step Guide to Relationship Mapping

1. List Key Relationships: Start by listing the people you interact with regularly. Include family members, friends, romantic partners, colleagues, and any others who significantly impact your emotional life.

2. Categorize the Relationships: Group these individuals based on the nature of your interaction—supportive, challenging, neutral. Use different colors or symbols for each category to differentiate them visually.

3. Assess the Impact of BPD Symptoms: Next to each name, note any specific BPD symptoms that frequently surface in that relationship. For example, you might write 'fear of abandonment' next to a partner or 'impulsivity' next to a friend with whom you often make spontaneous decisions.

4. Identify Patterns: Look for patterns in the map. Are there certain types of relationships where specific symptoms are more prevalent? Do supportive relationships help mitigate some BPD symptoms? This step is crucial for understanding how your BPD interacts with different social dynamics.

5. Evaluate Relationship Health: Reflect on each relationship's overall health. Consider how your BPD symptoms have affected the relationship and identify areas where you might work on improvement, such as building trust, enhancing communication, or setting boundaries.

Interpreting Patterns

- Recurrent Issues: If you notice the same issues appearing in multiple relationships, this might indicate areas where your BPD symptoms are most impactful. For example, if 'fear of abandonment' occurs frequently, it might suggest a need to work on security and self-confidence within close relationships.

- Support Systems: Relationships marked as supportive where symptoms are less impactful suggest these are healthy, stabilizing connections in your life.

This exercise is not just about identifying problems but also recognizing the strengths and supports already present in your life. By understanding the complex interplay between your relationships and BPD symptoms, you can begin to form strategies for improvement and foster healthier, more fulfilling connections.

BPD and Communication

Effective communication is a cornerstone of managing relationships impacted by Borderline Personality Disorder. Clear and mindful communication can significantly reduce conflicts and enhance mutual understanding. It helps bridge the gap between perceived threats and reality, allowing individuals with BPD and their loved ones to navigate the complexities of their interactions more smoothly.

For those with BPD, learning to express feelings and needs directly and respectfully can transform their relationships. It equips them to address issues before they escalate, fostering a climate of openness and trust. Furthermore, effective communication techniques also empower those around individuals with BPD to respond in ways that support emotional regulation rather than triggering further distress. By prioritizing clear dialogue, individuals with BPD can work towards building stability in their relationships, ensuring both parties feel heard and valued.

Mindful Communication

Mindful communication is a transformative approach that emphasizes being present and fully engaged during interactions. This method is especially beneficial for individuals with Borderline Personality Disorder, as it promotes understanding and patience in conversations, key areas often strained by the disorder's symptoms.

Practices of Mindful Communication

1. Mindful Listening: This involves listening to understand, not to respond. It requires you to focus entirely on the speaker, observing their words, tone, and body language without forming judgments or interruptions. By doing so, you can grasp the true essence of what is being communicated, which is crucial for responding appropriately and empathetically.

2. Mindful Speaking: Ensure your words are thoughtful and reflect genuine intent. This means considering the impact of your words before speaking and choosing those that foster clarity and kindness. Mindful speaking helps prevent misunderstandings and mitigates emotional reactions that could escalate conflicts.

Applying Mindful Communication

- Practice Active Listening: Show that you are listening by nodding, maintaining eye contact, and paraphrasing what the speaker has said to confirm understanding.

- Pause Before Responding: Take a moment to reflect on what has been said and how you feel. This pause allows you to respond from a place of calm rather than react impulsively.

- Address Barriers: Common barriers like comparing, mindreading, rehearsing, and judging can hinder effective communication. Recognize when these behaviors emerge and consciously steer the conversation back to a place of mindfulness.

By practicing mindful communication, which includes both listening and speaking mindfully, individuals with BPD and their loved ones can experience more meaningful and less contentious exchanges. This approach improves individual relationships and enhances overall emotional health, making everyday communications smoother and more enjoyable.

Activity: Interpersonal Effectiveness

Interpersonal effectiveness is a core component of Dialectical Behavior Therapy (DBT) that focuses on enhancing your ability to communicate and interact in relationships. Fundamental techniques like DEARMAN and GIVE are designed to help individuals with Borderline Personality Disorder improve their interactions through clear, assertive communication and maintaining positive relationships.

DEARMAN Technique DEARMAN is an acronym used to facilitate effective communication, especially when you need to make a request or assert yourself in a conversation:

- Describe: Explain the situation clearly and concisely. Use factual information.

- Express: Share your feelings and opinions about the situation using "I" statements.

- Assert: Clearly state what you want or do not want. Be direct and honest.

- Reinforce: Explain the positive effects of getting what you want or need. This may encourage the person to respond favorably.

- Mindful: Maintain your focus on your objectives. Do not be distracted or go off-topic.

- Appear confident: Use a confident tone and body language.

- Negotiate: Be willing to give to get. Offer and ask for alternative solutions if your request is denied.

GIVE Technique GIVE is used to maintain relationships and ensure interactions are respectful and considerate:

- Gentle: Be courteous and temper your approach, avoiding attacks or judgmental statements.

- Interested: Show interest in the other person's feelings and needs. Listen actively.

- Validate: Acknowledge the other person's feelings, wants, difficulties, and opinions. Validation shows you understand them, even if you do not agree.

- Easy Manner: Use humor, smile, and ease the tension when appropriate, making the conversation light and cooperative.

Applying These Techniques

These techniques can be used in everyday scenarios, such as resolving conflicts, asking for help, or expressing your needs. For example, using DEARMAN, you could effectively negotiate a compromise with a colleague, while GIVE might help maintain harmony during a difficult family discussion.

Incorporating DEARMAN and GIVE into your daily interactions promotes understanding and respect, significantly improving the quality of both personal and professional relationships. Diagrams or quick reference cards summarizing these steps can be helpful tools to remind you of the critical points during conversations.

Building on the interpersonal skills developed in this chapter, we now transition to exploring how these essential communication techniques and relationship strategies apply in a professional environment. The forthcoming chapter will delve into navigating workplace relationships, where the ability to handle interactions effectively can significantly impact career success and job satisfaction. By applying the DEARMAN and GIVE techniques, individuals with BPD can enhance their professional relationships, creating a more supportive and productive work atmosphere. This next chapter will provide targeted strategies to leverage your improved interpersonal effectiveness within the unique dynamics of the workplace.

Chapter Seven
Thriving at Work

Individuals with Borderline Personality Disorder possess the potential to achieve remarkable success in their careers by harnessing their unique strengths and mastering effective workplace strategies. The professional environment, with its structured routines and potential for achievement, offers a powerful platform for individuals with BPD to apply their intense passion and creativity. This chapter focuses on equipping you with fundamental techniques for self-advocacy, emotional regulation, and goal-setting—essential tools for not just surviving but thriving in the workplace.

Despite the challenges that BPD may present, such as navigating intense emotions and maintaining consistent professional relationships, there are proven strategies that can transform these potential obstacles into opportunities for personal and professional growth. By learning to effectively manage workplace dynamics through clear communication, time management, and self-reflection, individuals with BPD can leverage their profound capacities for empathy and resilience to build rewarding careers. The following sections will guide you through understanding the specific challenges BPD may bring into the workplace and provide practical, actionable strategies to address them, setting the stage for success in any professional endeavor.

BPD in the Workplace

Navigating the workplace with Borderline Personality Disorder presents unique challenges. The professional setting can trigger BPD symptoms like emotional sensitivity, fear of rejection or criticism, and fluctuating self-image, which can complicate interactions with colleagues and supervisors. Additionally, the tendency for "splitting"—viewing people and situations in black and white—can lead to conflicts and miscommunications.

This section thoroughly explores these workplace challenges, offering insights into how individuals with BPD can manage their symptoms effectively to maintain productivity and foster positive working relationships. Understanding these dynamics is the first step toward crafting a supportive and successful career environment.

Detailing Specific Challenges

Individuals with Borderline Personality Disorder often face heightened sensitivity to criticism, difficulties in maintaining professional detachment, and mood instability, which can significantly impact their workplace performance and relationships. These challenges, compounded by the symptom of "splitting," where individuals may perceive colleagues or situations as entirely good or bad, require nuanced strategies to manage effectively.

Sensitivity to Criticism

For someone with BPD, a simple critique can feel like a profound rejection or personal attack, triggering intense emotional responses. This sensitivity can lead to overreactions that may appear disproportionate to the situation, potentially alienating coworkers or supervisors.

According to a study published in the Journal of Personality Disorders, individuals with BPD often interpret neutral faces as angry or hostile, which can explain some of the difficulties they experience in response to feedback.

Professional Detachment

Maintaining an appropriate level of emotional detachment is challenging for individuals with BPD, who may form very intense emotional connections with others quickly. This tendency can blur professional boundaries, leading to complications in the workplace, especially in supervisor-subordinate relationships.

Moodiness

The emotional lability associated with BPD—rapid, intense, and often unpredictable mood shifts—can be confusing and difficult for colleagues to understand and accommodate. These mood changes can disrupt team dynamics and complicate collaborative projects, as coworkers may find it hard to adapt to the shifting emotional landscape.

Splitting

"Splitting," a symptom where individuals with BPD might alternate between idealizing and devaluing team members, can create divisions within the workplace. This behavior can lead to conflict and instability. Understanding and addressing this symptom is crucial for fostering a cooperative work environment. A study referenced on BorderlineIntheACT.org.au highlights how BPD can affect workplace relationships and emphasizes the importance of targeted support and understanding from HR and management.

Navigating these challenges requires awareness, self-regulation, and, often, professional guidance. Encouraging open communication about one's needs and limitations, as well as seeking therapy or counseling, can help mitigate these issues. Employers can also play a role by fostering an inclusive and supportive environment that accommodates the unique needs of employees with BPD, ultimately benefiting the entire organization.

Guide: Advocating for Yourself at Work

Self-advocacy in the workplace is a vital skill, particularly for individuals with Borderline Personality Disorder, who may require specific accommodations to optimize their work environment and performance. Advocating effectively starts with understanding your rights, recognizing your needs, and communicating these in a way that is both professional and respectful.

Getting in the Right Mindset

Begin by acknowledging your value as an employee and the unique strengths you bring to your role. Understanding that you deserve a supportive work environment is the first step towards effective self-advocacy. It's vital to approach advocacy with a mindset of seeking solutions that benefit both you and your employer rather than as a list of demands.

Understanding Your Rights

Familiarize yourself with workplace rights under laws such as the Americans with Disabilities Act (ADA), if applicable, which mandates reasonable accommodations for employees with disabilities, including mental health conditions like BPD. This might include flexible work hours, the ability to work from home, or changes to how feedback and instructions are given.

Identifying Your Needs

Reflect on aspects of your job that might be challenging due to BPD symptoms. For instance, if high stress triggers adverse reactions, consider what changes could help manage your stress. This might be regular breaks, a quiet workspace, or the option to have written summaries of meetings to avoid miscommunications.

Communicating Your Needs

When you're ready to discuss accommodations, plan what you'll say beforehand. Outline your needs clearly and explain how this will help improve your productivity and job satisfaction. For example, you might say, "Having the flexibility to start my day later helps me manage my sleep issues, which improves my concentration."

Documenting Your Advocacy

Keep records of your requests and any responses. Documentation can be helpful if you need to follow up or make additional requests. It also provides a clear trail of communication that can help prevent misunderstandings.

Building a Support Network

Rely on your professional network for support and advice. This might include trusted colleagues, mentors, or an experienced advocate from HR. They can offer guidance on how to navigate complex situations and may also help advocate on your behalf.

Examples of Effective Self-Advocacy

For instance, an employee with BPD might arrange a meeting with their supervisor to discuss how their condition affects their work and propose practical solutions, such as:

- Requesting to work on projects that allow for more independent work if interpersonal dynamics are challenging.

- Suggesting regular feedback sessions that are structured and written to reduce the stress of ambiguity and criticism.

Effective self-advocacy is about creating an environment where you can perform your best. Taking proactive steps to understand and articulate your needs empowers you to build a more supportive and productive workplace.

Tips: Time Management

Effective time management is crucial for enhancing both mental health and productivity, particularly for individuals with Borderline Personality Disorder. Mastering how to structure your day can mitigate stress and promote a more stable work environment. Here are practical strategies to help you manage your time efficiently, ensuring you meet your professional goals and support your mental well-being.

- Establish a Consistent Morning Routine: Start your day with a routine that sets a positive tone. Whether it involves meditation, a brief walk, or a cup of tea, find activities that calm your mind and prepare you for the day ahead. A predictable morning reduces anxiety and increases your control over the day's events.

- Utilize Time Management Tools: Leverage tools like digital calendars, task management apps, or traditional planners to keep track of deadlines and appointments. Tools like Trello, Asana, or Google Calendar can help you visualize tasks and manage your workload effectively.

- **Prioritize Tasks:** Begin each day by identifying the most critical tasks. Use the Eisenhower Box technique, a simple decision-making tool that categorizes functions into four categories: urgent, important, not urgent, and not important. This helps you focus on what truly needs your attention first, reducing the overwhelming feeling of a cluttered to-do list. Consider searching online or consulting productivity resources for a visual guide or further explanation of the Eisenhower Box.

- Limit Multitasking: Focus on one task at a time. While multitasking might seem efficient, it often leads to decreased productivity and increased stress. Single-tasking helps maintain focus and produces higher-quality work.

- Set Clear Boundaries: Know when to say "no" and protect your time. Overcommitting can lead to stress and burnout. Be realistic about what you can handle, and don't hesitate to delegate tasks when possible.

- Incorporate Breaks: Schedule short breaks throughout the day to prevent burnout. Use this time to step away from your workspace, stretch, or do a brief mindfulness exercise. Regular breaks can refresh your mind and increase productivity.

- Reward Yourself: Set up a system to reward yourself for completing tasks or meeting goals. This could be as simple as a coffee break after a major task or a movie night after a successful project week. Rewards can boost your motivation and satisfaction with your work.

Implementing these time management tips can create a more balanced and productive workflow, significantly improving your ability to handle workplace demands while managing BPD symptoms.

Exercise: Career Reflection

Career reflection is a powerful tool for understanding how well your current job aligns with your personal goals and the unique challenges posed by Borderline Personality Disorder. This exercise uses guided questions to help you delve deeply into your professional experiences, assess your satisfaction, and plan for future aspirations. Reflecting on these questions can provide valuable insights into how your BPD traits may influence your career choices and workplace interactions.

Reflective Questions to Guide Your Career Path

1. What aspects of your current job do you find most fulfilling?

2. Consider which tasks or responsibilities bring you joy or a sense of accomplishment. Identifying these can help clarify what to seek or enhance in your career.

3. Are there elements of your job that consistently trigger stress or negative emotions related to your BPD?

4. Recognize patterns where work might be exacerbating your symptoms. Understanding these triggers can be crucial in thinking about necessary changes or supports.

5. How do your BPD traits affect your professional relationships?

6. Reflect on both the positive and negative impacts. This might include challenges in teamwork, conflicts, or how your emotional intensity influences collaborations.

7. What skills or resources do you need to improve your professional situation?

8. Consider both personal development and external resources like training or workplace accommodations that could help you manage your BPD symptoms more effectively at work.

9. Where do you see your career in the next five years, and what steps can you take to reach those goals?

10. Setting long-term goals can provide a career roadmap, helping motivate and guide your professional decisions.

11. How can you align your career goals with your management of BPD?

12. Think about how your career decisions can support your health and well-being. This might involve seeking roles that offer greater flexibility, stability, or a supportive environment.

Use these questions to explore your current career trajectory and to identify changes that may enhance both your professional satisfaction and your management of BPD. Periodically reflecting on these questions can also help you track your progress and adjust your goals as needed to ensure they continue to serve your best interests and health.

Plan: Setting Career Goals That Align with Your Strengths

Setting career goals that align with your strengths is motivating and essential for long-term success, especially when managing Borderline Personality Disorder. This section guides you through identifying your strengths and setting realistic, fulfilling career goals considering your unique challenges and capabilities.

Identifying Your Strengths

Start by taking stock of your strengths. These can be skills you naturally excel at or traits that have consistently supported your personal and professional growth. Consider the following checklist to help pinpoint these strengths:

- Communication Skills: Are you good at expressing ideas, or do you excel in listening and understanding others' points of view?

- Creativity: Are you skilled at finding innovative solutions to problems and thinking outside the box?

- Resilience: Can you bounce back from setbacks with a stronger resolve to push forward?

- Empathy: Are you able to understand and share the feelings of others, making you a great team player or leader?

- Detail-Oriented: Do you have a knack for spotting errors and maintaining quality in your work?

Reflect on instances where these strengths have come into play in your work life and consider how they might be leveraged more effectively.

Setting Career Goals

With a clear understanding of your strengths, you can now set goals that are not only achievable but also inspiring. Use these tips to frame your goal-setting process:

- Be Specific: Define clear, specific goals. Instead of "advance my career," replace it with "obtain a managerial position by the end of next year."

- Consider Management of Your BPD Symptoms: Align your goals with your mental health needs. For instance, if regular schedules help manage your symptoms, look for or create roles that allow a consistent routine.

- Set Short and Long-Term Goals: While having long-term aspirations is excellent, short-term goals can provide quick wins and steady motivation.

- Write Them Down: Documenting your goals can help solidify them and make them feel more tangible.

- Plan for Challenges: Identify potential obstacles and consider how to overcome them. This might involve additional training, seeking mentorship, or adjusting work environments.

Remember, your career goals should excite and challenge you, pushing you toward greater fulfillment. They should also be flexible enough to adapt as your circumstances and abilities evolve. By aligning your professional aspirations with your strengths and considering your BPD management, you are setting a foundation for lasting satisfaction and success in your career.

Having explored the strategies for professional success, we now focus on broader coping mechanisms that underpin effective management of Borderline Personality Disorder. The skills developed in the workplace—such as self-advocacy, emotional regulation, and strategic planning—are valuable in a professional context and essential components of comprehensive BPD management. In the next chapter, we will delve deeper into these skills, expanding on how they can be adapted and applied across various aspects of daily life to foster resilience and promote overall well-being. This integrated approach aims to empower you with a robust toolkit for navigating life with BPD.

Chapter Eight
Coping Strategies

Effective coping strategies can significantly mitigate the intense and often overwhelming emotions common in Borderline Personality Disorder. This transformation is crucial for those managing the unpredictability of BPD, enabling them to lead more stable and fulfilling lives. This chapter delves into a comprehensive toolkit designed to provide immediate relief in acute distress and foundational practices for sustained well-being.

This chapter arms you with a diverse set of tools by exploring various techniques, from grounding exercises for quick calm to establishing routines that enhance emotional stability. Each strategy is tailored to fit into a personal coping toolkit, helping to smooth the emotional spikes and dips of BPD. Whether you're seeking quick solutions for sudden emotional surges or building a lifestyle conducive to long-term equilibrium, the guidance provided here aims to equip you with the skills necessary to turn daunting challenges into opportunities for growth and self-discovery. Prepare to explore how these coping mechanisms can serve as your allies in transforming how you experience and interact with the world around you.

Toolkit: Present Moment and Long-term Coping Strategies

Present Moment Strategies

In moments of acute distress, having a set of immediate coping strategies can be invaluable. These techniques are designed to quickly ground your emotions, helping you regain control and reduce the intensity of overwhelming feelings. Here's a breakdown of some effective methods:

- Grounding Techniques: Grounding helps distract your mind from distressing feelings by focusing on the present. Try the "5-4-3-2-1" method:

- Identify 5 things you can see.

- Notice 4 things you can touch.

- Listen for 3 sounds.

- Identify 2 things you can smell.

- Name 1 thing you can taste. This method brings your attention to your current environment and can be particularly useful during panic attacks or intense emotional episodes.

- **Distracting Activities:** Engage in activities that capture your full attention and divert it from distressing thoughts. This could be solving a puzzle, coloring, or playing a fast-paced game. These activities provide a temporary escape, giving your emotions time to settle.

- 1-Minute Mindfulness Exercises: Quick mindfulness exercises can center your thoughts and calm your mind. Try focused breathing for one minute, paying close attention to each breath, or silently naming items in your immediate vicinity to anchor yourself in the now.

- Creative Expression: Drawing, writing, or playing music allows you to express emotions in a constructive way. Artistic activities can lead to a state of flow, which is both therapeutic and calming.

- Connecting with Nature: Spending time in natural surroundings can have a profound calming effect. Activities like walking through a park, gardening, or simply sitting under a tree can help reduce stress and improve your mood.

Each of these strategies offers a practical approach to managing intense emotions rapidly and can be easily incorporated into your daily routine to help navigate moments of distress.

Long-term Strategies

For sustained emotional equilibrium, it is crucial to develop routines and form new habits that foster mental stability and wellness. Establishing structured daily routines and incorporating effective habit formation techniques can significantly enhance life quality for individuals with Borderline Personality Disorder.

Developing a Routine:

A consistent daily routine reduces uncertainty and helps manage anxiety, providing a predictable and safe framework to navigate daily life. Here's how to establish a beneficial routine:

- Morning Rituals: Start with a simple morning routine, such as meditation, a short walk, or a healthy breakfast, to set a positive tone for the day.

- Scheduled Breaks: Integrate regular breaks to rest and reset, which can prevent burnout and maintain productivity.

- Evening Wind-down: End the day with activities that promote relaxation, like reading, journaling, or a calming hobby, to ensure quality sleep.

Forming New Habits (Habit Stacking):

Habit stacking involves adding new habits to already established ones, making it easier to develop and maintain them. This method leverages the momentum of existing routines to incorporate new, beneficial behaviors seamlessly. For example:

- After brushing your teeth (existing habit), spend five minutes planning your day (new habit).

- While waiting for your morning coffee to brew, do a quick mindfulness exercise.

- Right before your regular lunch break, **take a moment to reflect or jot down what you're grateful for that day.**

The benefits of a structured routine and habit stacking include:

- Reduced Stress: Knowing what to expect each day can significantly lower stress levels.

- Improved Focus: A routine helps minimize distractions, keeping you more focused on the task at hand.

- Better Sleep: Regular sleep and wake times improve sleep quality, which is crucial for emotional and physical health.

- Increased Productivity: When your day is structured, you will likely achieve more with less effort.

Implementing these long-term strategies provides stability and builds a framework within which individuals with BPD can thrive, making daily challenges more manageable and improving overall life satisfaction.

Activity: Designing Your Personal Self-Care Kit

Creating a personal self-care kit is a proactive way to ensure you have tools at your disposal that can provide comfort and relief, especially during challenging times. This kit should be tailored to your sensory preferences and interests, offering a variety of items that can soothe and uplift you across all five senses. Here's how to curate a self-care kit that resonates with your personal needs and preferences.

1. Sight: Visually soothing items can have a calming effect. Consider including:

- Colorful Art Prints: Choose artwork that uplifts your spirits or brings you peace.

- Inspirational Quotes: Handwrite or print quotes that motivate and comfort you.

- Personal Photos: Family photos or pictures from happy times can boost your mood.

2. Sound: Sounds can dramatically affect your mood. Include items that produce or reproduce soothing sounds:

- Playlist of Calming Music: Assemble a list of music that relaxes or invigorates you.

- Nature Sounds: Apps or recordings that play sounds of rain, waves, or forest life can be immensely soothing.

- Miniature Musical Instruments: Such as a kalimba or a set of chimes can be both therapeutic and engaging.

3. Touch: Objects with pleasant textures can provide immediate comfort.

- Stress Balls or Fidget Toys: These can help manage anxiety and stress.

- Soft Blankets or Scarves: Items made from materials like fleece or cashmere offer comfort through their softness.

- Hand Cream or Massage Oils: These can provide a sensory experience that relaxes muscles.

4. Smell: Scents can have a powerful effect on mood.

- Essential Oils or Scented Candles: Lavender, chamomile, and sandalwood are known for their relaxing properties.

- Herbal Sachets: Small bags filled with dried lavender, mint, or your favorite herbs.

5. Taste: Sometimes, a little treat can go a long way in boosting your spirits.

- Favorite Snacks: Chocolate, dried fruits, or nuts can be comforting.

- Tea or Specialty Coffee: Include a selection of herbal teas or a small bag of your favorite coffee blend.

Building Your Kit:

- Choose a container like a decorative box, a backpack, or even a drawer in your home where you can keep these items. Make sure it is easily accessible whenever you need a moment of comfort or stress relief.

- • Personalize your kit. The more your self-care kit reflects your personality and needs, the more effective it will be. Consider decorating the container or including positive notes or affirmations to yourself.

Using Your Kit:

- Familiarize yourself with each item and remember why you chose it. Knowing exactly what to reach for during stressful moments and why it helps can make all the difference.

- Update your kit as your needs change. The effectiveness of your self-care tools might evolve, so it's important to keep the kit updated according to what works best for you currently.

Designing your personal self-care kit is not just about assembling items; it's about creating a collection of tools that you can access whenever you need stress relief, comfort, or a mood uplift. This kit will serve as a tangible resource to help maintain balance and manage symptoms of BPD, providing immediate support and ease when needed.

Reflection: Identifying and Replacing Unhealthy Coping Mechanisms

Recognizing and replacing unhealthy coping mechanisms with healthier alternatives is a pivotal step toward managing Borderline Personality Disorder effectively and improving overall well-being. This reflection encourages you to examine your current coping strategies and to consider more beneficial practices.

Common Unhealthy Coping Mechanisms:

- Substance Use: Turning to alcohol, drugs, or excessive caffeine as a quick escape from stress or emotional pain.

- Self-Harm: Engaging in self-injury as a physical outlet for emotional distress.

- Avoidance: Withdrawing from friends, family, and activities to avoid dealing with emotions or situations.

- Overeating or Under-eating: Using food as a comfort tool or not eating as a form of control.

- Overspending: Compulsively shopping to feel better temporarily.

Steps to Replace Unhealthy Coping Mechanisms:

1. Identify Triggers: Understand what situations, emotions, or people trigger your unhealthy coping behaviors. Awareness is the first step towards change.

2. Seek Healthy Alternatives: For each unhealthy mechanism, propose a healthy alternative. For example:

   - Substance Use → Physical Activity: Replace the impulse to use substances with going for a walk, doing yoga, or any physical activity you enjoy.

   - Self-Harm → Creative Expression: Channel painful emotions into art, writing, or music.

- ○ Avoidance → Structured Social Interaction: Plan regular, small gatherings with a supportive friend or family member.

- ○ Overeating/Under-eating → Mindful Eating: Focus on eating balanced meals at regular times and listening to your body's hunger cues.

- ○ Overspending → Budgeting: Set a budget for discretionary spending that allows for small treats without financial stress.

3. Implement Gradually: Start small and gradually incorporate these healthier alternatives into your life. Change takes time and patience.

Journal Prompts to Facilitate Self-Exploration:

- What emotions am I trying to avoid when I engage in unhealthy coping mechanisms?

- How do I feel after participating in these behaviors? Do they bring long-term relief or more distress?

- What are three healthy coping strategies I can start practicing this week?

- Who in my support network can help me maintain accountability as I replace these unhealthy behaviors?

Reflecting on these aspects of your behavior and writing down your thoughts can deepen your understanding and commitment to healthier coping strategies. This process not only supports your journey toward stability but also enhances your overall quality of life by fostering resilience and effective emotional management.

Positive Affirmations

Positive affirmations are a powerful tool for individuals with Borderline Personality Disorder to counteract the often automatic and intensely negative self-talk that can worsen their condition. These affirmations help rewire thought patterns, replacing critical or destructive thoughts with compassionate and empowering messages.

Understanding the Impact of Positive Affirmations

Affirmations reinforce self-worth and personal strength, which is essential for those with BPD who frequently battle feelings of worthlessness and insecurity. Regularly practicing positive affirmations can significantly influence emotional well-being, helping to stabilize mood fluctuations and boost resilience against everyday stressors.

Crafting Effective Affirmations for BPD

Affirmations should be personal, present tense, positive, and specific. They should align with your genuine aspirations and help strengthen your mental outlook. Here are examples tailored for BPD-related challenges:

- For Fear of Abandonment: "I am worthy of love and respect, even when I am alone."

- For Managing Emotions: "I control my emotions; they do not control me."

- For Self-Identity: "I am discovering more about who I am every day."

- For Interpersonal Relationships: "I deserve healthy, supportive relationships."

- For Self-Compassion: "I treat myself with kindness and patience."

Implementing Affirmations in Daily Life

To effectively integrate these affirmations into your life, follow these guidelines:

1. Consistent Practice: Repeat your affirmations daily. Morning routines are ideal as they help set a positive tone for the day.

2. Visualization: While reciting an affirmation, visualize yourself as embodying the statement. For instance, imagine interacting with others in a calm and confident manner.

3. Affirmation Placement: Place your affirmations where you will see them often—mirrors, computer monitors, or on your phone as a background.

4. Speak Aloud: Saying affirmations aloud increases their potency by engaging more of your senses and reinforcing their truth.

Customizing Your Affirmations

Personalize your affirmations to address your most pressing feelings or situations. Reflect on areas where you feel most vulnerable or unstable, and craft affirmations that directly support and empower you in those aspects.

Examples of Affirmations for Daily Use

- "Every day, in every way, I am becoming better and stronger."

- "I can achieve balance in my emotions and my life."

- "I handle my relationships with care and wisdom."

- "I am worthy of respect and understanding from others and myself."

- "I trust in my ability to navigate challenges successfully."

- "I embrace change and grow with every experience."

- "My thoughts create my reality, and I am the master of my thoughts."

Affirmations are not just phrases to repeat; they are commitments to change how you view yourself and interact with the world. By regularly using affirmations, individuals with BPD can cultivate a more positive mental arena, leading to improved stability and satisfaction in daily life.

As we transition from mastering personal coping strategies to understanding how to support someone with Borderline Personality Disorder, it's important to recognize that the insights gained from these strategies can enhance our ability to provide effective support. The next chapter is tailored specifically for individuals who interact closely with someone with BPD. It will explore how empathy, understanding, and appropriate interventions foster healthier relationships and provide significant support to the caregivers, helping them manage the challenges of this complex condition.

<u>Chapter Nine</u>
Supporting Someone with BPD

Supporting someone with Borderline Personality Disorder is a journey that requires a delicate balance of empathy, understanding, and self-care. This balance ensures that the support provided is effective and sustainable, benefiting both the supporter and the person with BPD. The challenges are real, and the emotional investment is significant. However, with the right tools and approaches, creating a supportive environment that fosters growth and stability for all involved is possible.

In this chapter, we dive into practical strategies and insights to help you offer support while maintaining your own well-being. From establishing healthy boundaries to mastering communication techniques that defuse tension, the guidance provided here aims to equip you with a comprehensive understanding of how best to support someone living with BPD. By focusing on empathy and clear, compassionate interaction, you will learn how to navigate the complexities of BPD, enhancing both your relationship and the emotional health of your loved one. This chapter serves as a guide to transforming challenges into opportunities for strengthening connections and fostering resilience.

Tips: How to Offer Support Without Burning Out

Providing support to someone with Borderline Personality Disorder is crucial, but it also requires a sustainable approach to avoid caregiver burnout. Sustainable support combines patience, understanding, and effective communication with crucial self-care strategies. These practices ensure that support helpers maintain their emotional and physical well-being while offering meaningful assistance. This section outlines practical tips for providing compassionate support without compromising one's health, enabling a balanced approach that benefits both the supporter and the individual with BPD.

Detailed Support Strategies

Supporting someone with Borderline Personality Disorder effectively involves a mix of empathy, clear communication, and self-preservation. Here, we explore detailed strategies to help maintain this balance, preventing burnout and enhancing the support provided.

- Be Patient: Patience is vital when dealing with BPD, as individuals may experience intense emotional fluctuations and fear of abandonment. Real-life example: If the person you are supporting reacts negatively to a seemingly minor issue, remember that their disorder often heightens their response. Respond with calmness and patience, acknowledging their feelings without escalating the situation.

- Don't Judge: Avoid judgmental comments or advice that sounds critical. People with BPD can be susceptible to criticism, and what seems like a small remark to you can be deeply hurtful to them. Practical tip: Use supportive language and focus on the behavior rather than the person. For instance, say, "I noticed you seemed upset yesterday," instead of "You overreacted yesterday."

- Set Clear Boundaries: Establishing and maintaining clear boundaries is crucial for both your well-being and that of the person with BPD. How to implement: Clearly communicate your limits in a respectful and firm manner. For example, if you need personal time, express it directly: "I care about you, but I need some time to myself this evening. Let's talk more tomorrow."

- Learn Their Triggers: Knowing what triggers emotional reactions in someone with BPD can help you anticipate and mitigate potential problems. Resource enhancement: Engage in open discussions about what situations or actions may trigger distress and explore ways to manage these triggers together.

- Provide Distractions: When emotions run high, simple distractions can help redirect the person's focus and reduce intensity. Suggested activities: Suggest a walk, a puzzle, or watching a favorite show together. These can offer a break from the stressful situation and help the person regain perspective.

- Learn More About BPD: Educating yourself about BPD will enhance your understanding and ability to provide practical support. Recommended reading: Resources such as Mind.org.uk's guide for friends and family and HelpGuide's article on helping someone with BPD provide valuable insights.

- Help Them Seek Treatment and Support: Encourage the person with BPD to seek professional help and support, which can be a cornerstone of managing the disorder. Actionable advice: Offer to help them research therapists or support groups or accompany them to an appointment if they are anxious about going alone.

- Take Care of Yourself: Supporting someone with BPD can be emotionally taxing, so it's essential to look after your own mental and physical health. Self-care strategies: Ensure you have time for activities you enjoy, seek support for yourself if needed, and don't hesitate to set emotional boundaries.

By integrating these strategies, you can offer compassionate, effective, and sustainable support, helping build a healthier relationship and promoting better outcomes for you and the person with BPD.

Exercise: Setting and Maintaining Healthy Boundaries

Establishing and maintaining healthy boundaries is essential when supporting someone with Borderline Personality Disorder. Effective boundaries help prevent feelings of resentment and burnout, and they ensure that both your needs and the needs of the person with BPD are respected.

Step-by-Step Guide to Setting Boundaries

1. Identify Your Limits: Reflect on what you can tolerate and accept versus what makes you feel uncomfortable or stressed. These feelings help identify where limits need to be set.

2. Clearly Communicate Your Boundaries: Use "I" statements to communicate your boundaries to avoid sounding accusatory or confrontational. For example:

- "I need some time to recharge myself. I will be unavailable after 8 PM each night."

- "I feel overwhelmed when discussions get heated. Let's agree to take a break and revisit the conversation when we are both calm."

1. Be Direct and Specific: Be as straightforward as possible about your boundaries, why they are necessary, and how you expect them to be respected. Avoid vague boundaries that are open to interpretation.

2. Prepare for Pushback: People with BPD may test boundaries, sometimes unintentionally. Prepare yourself to reassert your boundaries consistently if they are challenged.

3. Use Positive Reinforcement: When your boundaries are respected, acknowledge and appreciate them. This can reinforce the behavior and help build a positive relationship dynamic.

Maintaining Boundaries

- Consistency is Key: The importance of consistency cannot be overstated. Stick to your boundaries once you've set them. Inconsistent boundaries can create confusion and instability.

- Handle Violations Calmly: If your boundaries are violated, remind the person of your limits without escalating the situation. Use calm, clear communication to restate your boundary:

  - "Remember, I need some quiet time in the evenings. Let's plan to talk in the morning instead."

- Self-Check Regularly: Continually assess whether your boundaries are working or need adjustments. Check in with yourself about how you're feeling and whether you're beginning to feel resentful or stressed.

- Seek Support if Needed: Setting and maintaining boundaries can be challenging, especially when dealing with complex emotional dynamics associated with BPD. Don't hesitate to seek support from therapy groups or mental health professionals.

Practical Application

In a situation where the person with BPD is demanding more time and attention than you can provide, you might say:

- "I care about you and want to support you, but I also need to take care of my own needs. Let's find a specific time when I can give you my full attention."

Establishing and consistently maintaining boundaries supports your well-being and helps the person with BPD understand the framework of your relationship, leading to a healthier interaction for both parties.

Dialogue: How to Talk to Someone with BPD

Effective communication with someone who has Borderline Personality Disorder is pivotal, especially in emotionally charged situations. The SET (Support, Empathy, Truth) communication technique is specifically designed to facilitate conversations that are compassionate, clear, and constructive. This method helps in maintaining a positive connection while also addressing complex topics.

Understanding the SET Technique

- Support: Show your support by affirming that you care and are committed to the relationship. This reassures the person with BPD of your involvement and intention to help.

- Example: "I want to understand what you're going through because I care about you."

- Empathy: Empathy involves trying to understand the other person's feelings from their perspective and acknowledging their emotions. This validation can be profoundly soothing and can de-escalate intense emotions.

  - Example: "It sounds like you're really overwhelmed by this. I can see why that would be upsetting."

- Truth: Communicate the truth about your feelings and the situation in a gentle but honest manner. It's important to be honest without being critical or dismissive of their feelings.

  - Example: "I know it's hard, and I want to support you, but I also need us to think about solutions that work for both of us."

Applying the SET Technique in Conversations

1. Begin with Support: Always start by reinforcing your support for the person. This sets a positive tone and opens up the lines of communication.

   - "I care about you a lot, and I'm here to help us figure this out together."

- Express Empathy: Make it clear that you are trying to understand their feelings or situation from their perspective. This shows respect for their experience.

  - "I see this is really hard on you, and I understand why you might feel that way."

1. Speak Your Truth: Clearly state your perspective or needs. Be honest but considerate in how you communicate your message.

   ○ "While I want to help as much as possible, I also need us to find a way that doesn't leave me feeling overwhelmed."

Using SET in Difficult Conversations

Imagine a scenario where tensions are high. Maybe the person with BPD feels criticized or misunderstood. Using the SET technique might look something like this:

- Support: "I want to help you through this, not make it harder."

- Empathy: "I can see why you felt hurt when I brought this up."

- Truth: "It wasn't my intention to hurt you. Let's try to find a solution together."

By incorporating the SET technique into your conversations, you can improve communication effectiveness, enhance understanding, and foster a healthier relationship dynamic with someone who has BPD. This approach addresses immediate issues and builds a foundation of trust and mutual respect essential for long-term relationship stability.

As we conclude our exploration of supporting someone with Borderline Personality Disorder, it's essential to reflect on the journey we've embarked upon throughout this workbook. From understanding BPD's complexities, developing personal coping strategies, and effectively communicating and setting boundaries, each chapter has been designed to provide you with tools and knowledge to navigate this challenging situation.

The insights and strategies discussed aim to empower not only those directly affected by BPD but also their supporters, fostering environments of empathy, understanding, and growth. We've learned about the importance of self-care, the effectiveness of structured communication like the SET technique, and the critical role of setting and respecting boundaries to ensure that the help provided is both sustainable and beneficial.

Conclusion

This workbook has been a journey toward empowerment, equipping you with practical knowledge and strategies to manage Borderline Personality Disorder. Whether you are navigating this path personally or supporting someone who is, the tools and insights provided aim to enhance understanding and foster skill development. We've explored a variety of approaches—from coping mechanisms and communication techniques to setting boundaries and building resilience. The goal has been to empower you to transform challenges into opportunities for growth and to encourage a proactive stance in managing BPD for a more stable and fulfilling life.

Throughout this workbook, several fundamental insights have emerged that are vital for managing Borderline Personality Disorder effectively. First, self-awareness is crucial; understanding your own triggers and emotional patterns is the foundation for personal growth and better management of BPD. Secondly, the development of robust coping mechanisms—ranging from mindfulness exercises to structured routines—provides practical tools to handle stress and emotional upheavals. Lastly, nurturing supportive relationships is essential for receiving empathy and understanding and creating a network that fosters long-term stability and optimism. Together, these elements form a robust framework for navigating BPD with confidence and positivity.

This workbook is designed to be your ongoing companion toward managing Borderline Personality Disorder. As you face new challenges or when old issues resurface, revisit the strategies and exercises that have been most effective for you. Each section is crafted to adapt to your evolving needs, offering continued support and guidance. Keep moving forward, applying and refining the techniques you've learned.

If you've found this workbook helpful, please consider leaving a review. Your feedback can help others in their journey with Borderline Personality Disorder feel supported and understood.

It's quick, easy, and can make a significant difference to others.

review link: https://amzn.to/3ZhnFkE

*or scan here to leave a
review*

Thank you for contributing to our community's growth and for helping us better serve you and others.

References

- American Psychiatric Association. (2013). *Diagnostic and statistical manual of mental disorders* (5th ed.). American Psychiatric Publishing.

- National Center for Biotechnology Information. (n.d.). Borderline Personality Disorder. Retrieved from https://www.ncbi.nlm.nih.gov/books/NBK430883/

- Polaris Teen Center. (n.d.). Borderline Personality Disorder in Teens. Retrieved from https://polaristeen.com/articles/borderline-personality-disorder-in-teens/

- Verywell Mind. (n.d.). How Borderline Personality Disorder Affects Marriage. Retrieved from https://www.verywellmind.com/borderline-personality-and-marriage-425222#citation-1

- ResearchGate. (n.d.). Employment in Borderline Personality Disorder. Retrieved from https://www.researchgate.net/publication/232278883_Employment_in_Borderline_Personality_Disorder

- Change Mental Health. (n.d.). Money Worries and Mental Health. Retrieved from https://changemh.org/resources/money-worries-and-mental-health/#

- The Mighty. (n.d.). What Not to Say to a Friend with BPD. Retrieved from https://themighty.com/topic/borderline-personality-disorder/what-not-to-say-to-friend-with-bpd-borderline-personality/

- BPD Carers Sanctuary. (n.d.). Glossary. Retrieved from https://bpd-carers-sanctuary.org/glossary/

- The Mighty. (2022, May). Borderline Personality Disorder Glossary for New Diagnosis. Retrieved from https://themighty.com/2022/05/borderline-personality-disorder-glossary-new-diagnosis/

- Rethink Mental Illness. (2023, July). Living with Borderline Personality Disorder: Rachel's Story. Retrieved from https://www.rethink.org/news-and-stories/blogs/2023/07/living-with-borderline-personality-disorder-rachels-story/

- National Alliance on Mental Illness. (n.d.). My Struggle With Borderline Personality Disorder. Retrieved from https://www.nami.org/Personal-Stories/My-Struggle-With-Borderline-Personality-Disorder

- Rethink Mental Illness. (2021, May). BPD Impacts My Life in Every Way: Gabby's Story. Retrieved from https://www.rethink.org/news-and-stories/blogs/2021/05/bpd-impacts-my-life-in-every-way-gabby-s-story/

- National Alliance on Mental Illness. (n.d.). Borderline Personality Disorder. Retrieved from https://www.nami.org/About-Mental-Illness/Mental-He

alth-Conditions/Borderline-Personality-Disorder

- Rancho Milagro Recovery. (n.d.). Challenges That Come with Borderline Personality Disorder. Retrieved from https://ranchomilagrorecovery.com/challenges-that-come-with-borderline-personality-disorder/

- Group Therapy. (n.d.). SMART Goals for Borderline Personality Disorder. Retrieved from https://www.grouporttherapy.com/blog/smart-goals-for-borderline-personality-disorder

- Dialectical Behavior Therapy | Connections Wellness Group. **https://connectionswellnessgroup.com/services/dialectical-behavior-therapy-program-texas/**